My story began when I was seven years old, living in Howard Beach,Queens. Though I couldn't understand it fully at the time, the events that unfolded would go on to shape the course of my life in ways I could never have imagined. As a young boy, I felt powerless in the face of what was happening, and for many years, I carried the burden of believing I was somehow responsible for the outcome of those events. But after much reflection and struggle, I've come to understand that I had no more control over those circumstances than any other child. I've come to realize that in order to move forward in my life, I must finally release the grip this past had on me.

Since you are reading this, I ask you to approach these pages with an open heart and mind, knowing that this is a story of vulnerability, struggle, and ultimately, of resilience. It is a story that I've carried for a lifetime, and it is time to let it go.

Chapter 1

Welcome to Howard Beach, Queens

For a seven-year-old boy from Glendale Court, Brooklyn, the drive to Howard Beach, Queens, felt like an adventure. The streets of Queens, with their busy intersections and bustling sidewalks, flew past the car windows adding to the anticipation. Beside me, my father, Harold, gripped the wheel with a quiet confidence. We shared a rare, unspoken smile, the kind that comes from a shared sense of purpose. This journey wasn't just another drive; it was the start of something new, something big.

For my father, this was more than a move. After years of toiling in the restaurant business, he had finally made it—he owned his own coffee shop and bought his first house. I could sense his excitement, a rare emotion for a man who usually kept his feelings locked away. As we neared our new home, he made eye contact with me, something that didn't happen often. His communication was usually limited to a nod or a finger point, but today, there was more behind those eyes.

"Do you think the new house will be nice?" I asked, trying to break the silence that had settled between us. He glanced over, gave me a quick smile, and nodded affirmatively. It wasn't much, but it was enough. I didn't push for more; I was just happy to be with him, to be part of this moment.

My father had always been distant, a man of few words and even fewer expressions of affection. There were no grand gestures, no hugs, or words of encouragement. Instead, his love was shown in small, easily overlooked moments. During our drives, in an era before wearing seat belts became standard, he had a habit of throwing his arm across my chest whenever he had to brake suddenly. It was a simple, instinctive move, but to me, it was everything. That brief contact, that moment of protection, was his way of showing he cared. These moments, though fleeting, were the closest he came to expressing affection. And in those small gestures, I felt his love, a love that was as quiet and restrained as the man himself. It was a warmth that lingered long after the drive was over, a symbol of his presence in my life.

At home, my mother Helen, struggled with severe depression and mental illness. The atmosphere was often heavy with the weight of her struggles. My mother's battle with severe depression and mental illness created a pervasive sense of unease that seemed to seep into every corner of our lives.

The household, meant to be a sanctuary, felt more like a stormy sea with no clear horizon. The atmosphere at home was constantly fraught with tension. Strained, stretched thin by the unpredictability of my mother's moods and the depth of her despair.

As we approached 163rd Avenue and 90th Street in Howard Beach, I could sense an unusual excitement emanating from my father. Today was special; it marked a milestone that he had longed for—a moment of personal triumph and new beginnings. This was going to be his first home, a symbol of hard work and dreams realized.

The street was abuzz with activity. The commotion was due to workmen laying down fresh asphalt, a sign that the area was being prepared for new residents.

We parked the car on the corner. Stepping out, the air was filled with the smell of wet cement and asphalt, a distinct aroma of change and progress.

As we walked up the block on the newly poured sidewalk, the ground beneath our feet was still slightly damp. My father's steps were lighter, his demeanor full of pride and anticipation.

Each house stood in neat, identical rows, a mirror image of its neighbors with a front door walkway on the left and a single-car garage door on the right. The air was alive with the popping noises of hammers driving nails into rooftops. Workers moved with purpose, carrying plywood on their backs while landscapers unrolled sod to create instant green lawns, transforming the raw, new development into a burgeoning neighborhood.

Amid this activity, the sight of the big steam roller captured my attention like nothing else. It was a massive machine, its sheer size and purpose both awe-inspiring and slightly intimidating. I watched from the sidewalk, mesmerized by the way steam radiated from the freshly laid asphalt, creating a shimmering effect that made the street look dangerously hot. As the steam roller rolled past, two workers casually crossed the street behind it, seemingly unfazed by the roaring machine. Their calm demeanor suggested that the area was safe, and their presence added a layer of normalcy to the otherwise dramatic scene.

Feeling emboldened by the workers' casual approach, I decided to take a closer look. I glanced over at my father, who was deep in conversation with the building foreman. It was clear that he was engrossed, leaving me a moment of freedom to explore.

Feeling the warmth of the asphalt through my shoes, I took a tentative step forward. The heat radiating from the ground was intense but not unbearable, adding to the thrill of my small adventure. My sense of wonder grew. I watched as the machine went back and forth, fascinated by its power and precision.

The construction site was alive with sound and motion, and I felt a sense of connection to the transformation happening around me. There didn't seem to be any immediate danger—everything looked and felt intriguing rather than alarming. If anything, I thought, this was going to be fun. With a determined step, I walked down the middle of the street, my eyes fixed on the steamroller ahead.

As I drew closer, the roar of the machine grew louder, its vibrations faintly felt through the ground. I approached cautiously, stopping just a few feet behind the steamroller. I marveled at its sheer size and the way it seemed to dominate the street with its power. As the steamroller roared back to life, I found myself caught up in its rhythmic progress. I marched just behind the massive machine, matching my steps to the steady, mechanical pace. My eyes followed the steam and water that washed over the big steel wheel, the liquid shimmering as it splashed onto the freshly laid asphalt. Each pass of the wheel was accompanied by a dramatic burst of steam, which added to the sense of excitement and wonder. I kept close to the steamroller, feeling a mixture of exhilaration and cautious curiosity. For a while, I managed to stay right behind it, my pace synchronized with its methodical progress.

Then, without warning, the steamroller came to an abrupt halt. The sudden stop was jarring, and I found myself only a few feet away from the colossal machine. The immediate cessation of motion left a heavy silence in the air, the roar of the engine replaced by the distant sounds of construction and the steady hum of nearby power saws. I stood there, momentarily stunned by my close proximity to the steamroller.

As I stood and waited, something shiny caught my eye to the right of the wheel's path. I slowly moved over to investigate, trying to identify the object now embedded in the asphalt. The gleaming reflection against the dark surface intrigued me, drawing me closer. Just as I focused intently on the mysterious object, a sudden spray of hot water hit the back of my neck. The unexpected warmth made me flinch and react instinctively. I jumped away from the hot mist, looking back over my shoulder to see the enormous wheel rolling past me, its sheer size and weight now more intimidating than ever.

The steamroller's reverse movement created a gust of steam and hot water that enveloped the area where I had just been standing. The sudden shift of the machine and the scalding spray heightened my sense of urgency and danger. My pulse raced as I scrambled to a safer distance, the world around me a blur of motion and sound. The steamroller continued its slow, deliberate reverse, and I stood there, trembling with a mix of fear and adrenaline. The shiny object I had spotted in the asphalt, which moments ago had captured my attention, was now forgotten—replaced by the stark reality that I had just been inches away from a tragic fate.

My heart pounded in my chest as I turned to look at my father, who stood rooted to the sidewalk. His gaze was fixed on me, and our eyes met. In that instant, I saw something I had never seen before—a look of pure, unfiltered fear. My father's face was drained of all color, and his mouth hung open in a silent expression of shock. Seeing my father, normally so composed, so utterly rattled, sent a chill down my spine. The gravity of what had just happened hit me hard. I felt a wave of apprehension and relief as I slowly made my way back to the sidewalk, my legs unsteady beneath me. I braced myself for what I was sure would be a stern lecture, a verbal lashing that would match the severity of the scare I had given him. But as I approached, I noticed that my father was struggling to find his voice. When he finally spoke, it was in a raspy whisper. "Don't tell your mother.

Chapter 2

The Hidden Talent

Shortly after we moved into our new home in that summer of 1965, life began to settle into its new rhythm. With school on the horizon, I was enrolled and started adjusting to the routine of a new environment.

During that summer, my father's brother Bernie paid us a visit along with his wife Harriet and their two children, Marlene and Roger. Marlene and Roger were already in high school, appearing to be around thirteen or fourteen years old. Their presence added a touch of familiarity amid the changes, but the visit was fleeting.

After this initial visit, I have no recollection of Bernie and his family coming to see us again after that summer. In fact, my family never made the effort to visit Bernie and his family at their home either. The connection that had once seemed promising appeared to dwindle into silence.

The remainder of my summer turned into a psychological struggle, a battle I hadn't anticipated. Each day seemed to bring new challenges, but the most difficult of all was dealing with my mother. Our interactions, once marked by a semblance of normalcy, had become increasingly volatile. It seemed as though her temper could flare at the slightest provocation, turning even the simplest conversations into minefields. I found myself walking on eggshells, never quite sure what might set her off. The unpredictability of her moods left me constantly on edge, bracing for the next outburst.

The house began to feel like a battleground. I felt myself retreating further into my own thoughts, trying to shield myself from the storm that had become our daily life. It was a struggle to maintain any sense of stability, and the joy that summer typically brought was overshadowed by the tension that filled our home. I found myself clinging to the thought of the upcoming school year. The first day of school was no longer just a date on the calendar—it had become a beacon of hope. The idea of meeting new people, of being in a different environment where I could be just another kid, was a welcome thought. It was a chance to start fresh, to carve out a place for myself away from the struggles that had defined my summer.

One Saturday morning I recall wandering through the house, searching for my father. His car was parked in the driveway, but he was nowhere to be found. The house seemed unusually quiet. A faint melody caught my attention, drifting up from the basement.

I made my way down the wooden steps creaking softly under my weight. The music grew louder, a gentle accompaniment to the scene that awaited me at the bottom. Upon reaching the basement, my eyes were drawn to my father, who was deeply engrossed in a surprising endeavor. He was seated in front of an easel, a palette of paints held deftly in one hand while the other guided a brush across a canvas.

I stood silently, watching my father as he immersed himself in his painting. The quiet focus he brought to his work made me realize that he, too, needed an escape from my mother's undiagnosed insanity. Her volatile moods affected everyone in the house, and it became clear to me that my father had found his refuge in his art. His love for painting wasn't just a hobby; it was a lifeline, a way to maintain his sanity in a world that could be chaotic and unpredictable. The quiet environment he created for himself while working was more than just a preference—it was a necessity. It allowed him to block out the noise, to find peace and focus in the midst of the storm. As I stood there, I couldn't help but think that his retreat into painting was not just about creating art, but about preserving a part of himself that could easily be lost in the chaos of our home. It was a reminder that we all needed our own ways to cope, to find peace, even in the most difficult circumstances.

My father glanced up from his work, his expression a mix of concentration and quiet satisfaction. He acknowledged me with a brief nod, a gesture that seemed to say, "I see you, and this is what I'm doing." There was no need for words; the moment spoke volumes. I remained there for a while, absorbing the quiet intensity of the scene. The discovery of my father's hidden talent marked a turning point for me, a glimpse into a side of him that had been previously unknown to me. The beauty of the painting and his calm focus offered me a new perspective on my father, forever altering my understanding of the man who had always been somewhat distant and enigmatic.

I was captivated by the painting I had discovered in the basement, and I returned the next day, eager to see how my father's artwork would be completed.

One week later, my father presented me with a small canvas and a set of brushes. I was overwhelmed and excited as I took the gift. However, when I tried my hand at painting, the experience was frustrating. The brushes felt unwieldy, and despite my best efforts, I couldn't quite achieve the results I wanted. The process of creating something positive with them eluded me.

One Sunday morning, like many others, my father followed his usual routine of picking up the New York Times. When he returned, we both sat down, the newspaper spread open between us, a silent invitation for me to join him in this weekly ritual.

As he began flipping through the pages, I watched his hands move methodically, the rustle of paper filling the room. His face was focused, absorbed in the search for the desired section. Then, with a sudden stop, he found what he was looking for. Without a word, he moved the paper toward me. I leaned in, curious to see what had caught his attention.

In front of me was a "color by number" page, its bold lines and numbered sections inviting creativity without requiring advanced skills. My father handed me a few colored pencils, their vibrant hues a promise of possibility. "Give this a try," he said with a smile, his encouragement genuine and warm. For me, this was a transformative moment. The simplicity of the color by number activity allowed me to engage in art without the frustration of mastering complex techniques. I carefully selected colors and began to fill in the numbered sections, each stroke bringing the image to life with a satisfying ease. This simple yet profound activity not only gave me a sense of accomplishment but also forged a new connection between me and my father. The moment was more than just a playful diversion; it was a bridge to understanding and a way to share in the joy of creativity.

The following weekend, my father turned to me with a grin and announced that we were going to visit the World's Fair. At seven years old, I didn't quite grasp the enormity of the event, but the mere promise of a day away from home with my father filled me with an eager anticipation.

As we drove towards Flushing Meadow Park in Queens, I could feel the excitement bubbling inside me. The sparkle in my father's eyes made it clear he was truly excited as well. This was more than just a trip; it was a chance to step into a world beyond our everyday routine, to explore, to dream, and to experience something that, at least for me, seemed to be filled with endless possibilities. Little did I know that this day would become a defining memory, a snapshot of time when the ordinary turned extraordinary.

The parking lot was a sea of vehicles, a labyrinth of metal and chrome, reflecting the bright summer sun as we navigated our way through. Each row seemed to blend into the next, and as we circled in search of a spot, the excitement in my chest grew, mingling with a hint of impatience. Finally, we found a space, and my father maneuvered the car into it, his hands steady on the wheel. With the car parked, we made our way towards the entrance of Flushing Meadow Park, where the grand structures of the World's Fair loomed in the distance. My father carried a brown camera bag, its leather worn from years of use. It held not only his camera but our lunch.

The bag swung lightly from his shoulder as we walked toward the entrance, surrounded by hundreds of other people who were just as excited as we were to enter the Fair. The entrance itself was a marvel—an archway that seemed to promise adventure and wonder beyond.

We joined the stream of visitors, their faces lit up with the same excitement that I felt. My father's camera bag was a small anchor in this sea of new experiences, a reminder that amid the spectacle, there was a shared purpose: to enjoy the day together, to explore, and for him to make memories that would last us a lifetime.

We eventually made our way to an exhibit that featured dozens of quirky machines, each promising a unique experience. The clamor of voices and the hum of excitement surrounded us, but I was drawn to one particular machine. It was a wax dinosaur maker, and its bright, colorful display promised to create a small, intricate dinosaur for just a quarter. My father fished a quarter from his pocket and popped it into the machine. As the gears whirred and the mechanical components came to life, I watched with bated breath. Slowly, the machine began to mold and shape the wax, crafting a small green Triceratops right before my eyes. The process was mesmerizing—a blend of art and technology that seemed almost magical.

When the wax dinosaur finally emerged, warm and slightly pliable, I could hardly contain my excitement. It was a perfect little Triceratops, its vibrant green hue and detailed features making it seem almost lifelike. I clutched it in my hand, marveling at the fact that such a tiny piece of magic could be created in just minutes. In that moment, surrounded by the fantastical attractions of the fair and the joy of a simple machine, I felt a profound connection—to the wonder of the day, to the bond with my father, and to the timeless thrill of discovering something new.

Despite my father's aversion to heights, he was determined not to let it dampen our adventure. We made our way to the observation tower, a structure that promised a panoramic view of the entire fairgrounds. I could see the excitement in my father's eyes, even though I knew he was apprehensive about the height. The tower had three levels, each offering a higher vantage point. As we ascended, the thrill of the view was palpable, but so was my father's visible discomfort. I could sense his unease, though he tried to mask it with a brave face. We decided to stay on the lowest observation level, the one that offered a sweeping view without being too overwhelming. From this vantage point, the fairgrounds sprawled out beneath us like a vibrant, living tapestry.

The colorful pavilions, the bustling crowds, and the gleaming exhibits created a mosaic of activity and excitement. I stood beside my father, looking out over the expanse with wide-eyed wonder, and I could see his anxiety gradually giving way to a sense of accomplishment.

As we descended back to solid ground, my father's relief was evident, but so was the satisfaction of having shared this experience.

The observation tower, with its heights and views, became a symbol of the day's adventure and the way we faced fears and found joy in each other's company. After our time on the observation tower, we wandered through the fairgrounds until my father spotted a bench nestled in a quieter corner, offering a welcome respite from the bustling crowds.

We both sat down, facing each other straddling the wooden bench. It was a simple, yet perfect spot to take a break and savor the moment. My father reached into his camera bag, pulling out two neatly wrapped sandwiches. He placed them on the bench between us, the familiar scent of fresh bread and fillings mingling with the faint aroma of the fair's many food stalls. My father purchased two large Cokes and placed them on the bench between us.

The fair buzzed with activity around us, but in that moment, the world seemed to pause. The distant hum of laughter, music, and carnival rides faded into the background, leaving just the two of us in a quiet oasis amid the excitement. As we unwrapped our sandwiches, there was an unspoken understanding between us, a shared appreciation for the simplicity of the moment.

The paper crinkled softly as we revealed the contents—nothing fancy, just good, honest food that seemed perfect for the occasion. We took a moment to enjoy the sight and smell before digging in. Our eyes met briefly, a subtle glance that carried the unspoken bond of father and son. It was in these small, everyday gestures that our connection was most evident. We reached for our sodas at the same time, the cold, fizzy drinks offering a refreshing contrast to the warmth of the summer day. My attention momentarily drifted, and my fingers lost their grip on the cup. In an instant, the soda, with its frothy bubbles and dark liquid, spilled from the cup and cascaded across the bench. Time seemed to slow as I watched in horror, the cold liquid and crushed ice flowing directly into the open crease of my father's loafers. He looked down at his shoe, now filled with a chilly mixture of Coke and ice, and then back at me. I felt a flush of embarrassment, my cheeks warming as I fumbled for words of apology.

My father's initial reaction was one of mild disgust as he stood up, his face displaying signs of frustration. He carefully removed his soda-drenched shoe, attempting to pour out the remaining liquid and ice that had pooled inside.

The sight of him wrestling with the sticky mess made me feel a pang of guilt. I followed closely behind, my steps quickening as I tried to offer help. The laughter and chatter of the fair seemed to fade into the background as I focused on the small disaster unfolding. My father, holding his damp shoe and moving with a slight, comical hobble, made his way towards the nearest restroom. Inside, he gingerly carried his drenched shoe, leaving a small trail of soda and ice behind him. The restroom, with its stark fluorescent lights and echoing tiles, felt like a stark contrast to the vibrant chaos of the fair outside.

As I watched, my father removed his wet sock and rinsed it out in the sink, the cold water helping to dilute the sticky residue of the spilled soda. The restroom was a blend of old and new, and one of the new features caught my eye—a hot air blower mounted on the wall, designed to dry hands quickly and efficiently.

With a hint of resourcefulness and a dash of good humor, my father approached the hot air blower, his wet shoe and sock in hand. I thought it was funny as he carefully placed the damp items under the stream of warm air, attempting to dry them as best he could. Balancing on one foot, his bare toes lifted off the cold, tile floor, he looked every bit the picture of determined improvisation.

The air blower's hum filled the small room, its warm breath offering some relief from the chill that had settled into his soaked footwear. Every now and then, the sound of the entrance door opening would mingle with the blower's drone, as new visitors entered and paused to witness the sight of my father's impromptu balancing act. Strangers watched with a mix of curiosity and amusement as my father performed his delicate dance, shifting his weight from side to side, trying to keep his balance.

It was one of those moments where the mundane turned into something memorable, a glimpse of the lighter side of a man who often carried the weight of the world on his shoulders. In that small, tiled room, with its cold floors and echoing footsteps, my father's quiet dance under the hot air dryer became a moment in my mind that will last forever.

Chapter 3

Unexpected Encounters

The crisp, cool air of fall had arrived, heralding the start of a new school year. The vibrant hues of autumn seemed to mirror the fresh start that awaited, offering a contrast to the tension and struggle that had defined my summer.

I was enrolled in P.S. 146 on 159th Avenue.

The camaraderie forged at the bus stop became a comforting constant; conversations flowed easily, punctuated by laughter and shared stories. These new friendships provided a sense of belonging, a way to navigate the unfamiliar terrain of a new school and neighborhood.

The familiarity of summer's warmth and freedom was replaced by the promise of new experiences and the structure of academic life.

A couple of months into the school year, my parents were invited to attend a parent-teacher conference. It was a routine meeting intended to discuss my progress and overall adjustment to the new school environment. However, the discussion took an unexpected turn.

As the teacher reviewed the general curriculum and my academic performance, she shifted to a more concerning topic: my behavior. She expressed unease about my tendency to be restless, easily distracted, and impulsive.

In 1965, what we now know as Attention Deficit Hyperactivity Disorder (ADHD) was not yet identified under this name. Instead, it was often categorized as "Hyperkinetic Impulse Disorder" or "Minimal Brain Dysfunction."

The teacher's concerns were a reflection of the period's evolving awareness of behavioral and learning disorders. While the terminology and understanding were rudimentary compared to contemporary standards, the underlying issue of my difficulties was being acknowledged for the first time.

For my parents, it was a moment of realization that my behavior was more than just a phase or a matter of poor discipline; it was an early indication of a condition that would only be more fully understood years later.

The conference left them with mixed feelings. They were faced with the challenge of navigating an educational system that was only beginning to grapple with the complexities of such disorders. It was the beginning of a journey through uncharted territory, where understanding and support would slowly evolve.

After the arrival of my younger brother, my mother's second child, that year her condition worsened significantly. The strain of the new baby, on top of her ongoing struggles, left her increasingly incapacitated. She was no longer able to provide even the most basic care or support for my brother and me. She spent most of her days in bed, unable to engage with the demands of daily life.

The weight of her depression and mental illness rendered her a silent and immovable presence that cast a heavy shadow over the household. As a result, I was left to navigate the challenges of my young life largely on my own. Each morning became a test of self-reliance. I had to get myself up for school, dress, and prepare my own breakfast. I often wore the same clothes for days on end, their wear and tear a testament to my neglect. My breakfast, a meager start to my day, typically consisted of candy or chewing gum—simple, sugary sustenance that I ate as I walked to the bus stop.

The conditions for my brother were equally dire. At just two years old, he spent long stretches of time sitting in a dirty diaper, his discomfort and distress manifesting in persistent, plaintive cries from his crib. It was as if he were trapped, a tiny prisoner in a space where his needs went unmet.

My father's coffee shop business demanded an early start. He was out of the house by 5:00 a.m. each day, a schedule that ensured he was absent from the household's daily struggles. This early departure was not just a necessity of his job but also a way to distance himself from the chaotic reality at home. He effectively remained out of sight and, more importantly, out of mind.

While his shop closed at 3:00 p.m., his return home was consistently delayed, often to 8:00 p.m. each evening. The extended hours away from home were a double-edged sword. On the one hand, they kept him removed from the immediate challenges and responsibilities of managing the household; on the other, he failed to see how his wife's mental health issues were building.

Meals, which should have been a source of nourishment and comfort, became a battleground. My mother's refusal to provide food was not necessarily tied to any specific transgression on anyone's part, but was rather a reflection of her deteriorating mental state. Her actions seemed more about her own convenience than any actual discipline. She would walk through the house, her voice echoing with a cruel chant, "You're starving, you're starving."

This daily ritual was a harsh and arbitrary form of punishment, driven not by my behavior but by my mother's need to impose her will. The refusal of meals became a tool of control and a way to simplify her own responsibilities, with one less meal to prepare and one less aspect of daily life to manage. For my brother and me, the lack of guidance and support was compounded by these regular acts of neglect. The emotional and physical toll was immense, as we faced each day with uncertainty.

Our home was situated just three blocks from Cross Bay Boulevard, the bustling main street lined with stores and eateries. For me, this proximity was a small but significant stroke of luck amid the hardships I faced at home. One of the nearest and most welcoming establishments was a restaurant called “-The Bow Wow.-” It quickly became my refuge. The Bow Wow was more than just a place to get a meal; it was a sanctuary where I could find a semblance of normalcy and comfort. Seventy cents would buy me a tuna sandwich, while thirty cents would get me an order of fries. The affordability made it possible for me to visit regularly, despite the limited resources at my disposal.

I had a small "piggy bank" hidden in my room, a repository for the spare change I managed to save. This piggy bank was a symbol of my independence and resourcefulness. Every coin added up to small but meaningful purchases that allowed me to sustain myself outside the confines of home. Every visit to “The Bow Wow” came with a small dilemma: should I splurge the additional thirty cents for fries, or should I save the money for future meals?

After finishing my sandwich, I often spent hours in the arcade, watching the other kids and hoping for a chance to join in their games. Though I rarely had enough spare change for the games, I found comfort in the atmosphere and the presence of other kids.

Despite my mother’s severe mental illness, she never received the evaluation or treatment she so desperately needed. It was evident to those around her, and to anyone observing her daily struggles, that her condition required professional intervention. Her symptoms were pronounced, and the turmoil they caused was undeniable. Yet, in a time when mental health issues were often stigmatized or misunderstood, my mother’s plight went unaddressed.

After reflecting on the discussion with my teacher, my mother devised a plan she believed would alleviate her own stress and simplify her life. While her plan might have appeared to offer short-term relief, its implications were far-reaching and ultimately destructive. She decided that I needed to be removed from the home and sent to an institution for children.

The plan hinged on convincing my father to agree to the move. My mother's strategy was straightforward—she knew that my father's detachment from the family dynamics made him a likely ally in this decision.

When she broached the subject with my father, she was calm and matter-of-fact. She presented the idea as a practical solution, framing it as a necessary step for my well-being and for the overall stability of the household. My father, already distanced from the family's day-to-day challenges, was swayed by the simplicity of the argument and the prospect of resolving the situation with minimal disruption to his own routine.

As my mother moved forward with her plan, the sense of betrayal and abandonment that I would experience loomed large. The decision to send me away, driven by a desire to ease my mother's own burden rather than address the underlying issues, marked a pivotal moment in my life. It was a decision that would sever my remaining ties to a semblance of family life and thrust me into an environment of institutional coldness, where the familiar warmth of home would be replaced by sterile walls and rigid schedules.

My mother wasted no time putting her plan into action. She made a few phone calls and arranged for me to be evaluated by a therapist, believing this step would provide the necessary justification for her decision. For her, the evaluation was a mere formality, a way to secure the professional endorsement she needed to move forward with her plan. She had little regard for the emotional toll that this decision would have on me.

Chapter 4

The Waiting Game

With the appointment just a few days away, my mother's focus was increasingly fixed on the imminent evaluation. Her calm demeanor was a contrast to the usual stress and turmoil that marked her days. The prospect of having the therapist's report validate her decision brought her a sense of relief and accomplishment.

My mother's daily routine was a reflection of her detachment from the world around her. She would rise from bed around noon, make herself a cup of instant coffee; with coffee in hand settle in by the television, spending hours lost in a sea of daytime programming. The television became a backdrop to her days, a constant presence in her increasingly disconnected existence.

Although the family's new home was impressive, it did come with a significant drawback: the need for a car to navigate beyond the confines of our residential area. For my mother, this posed a considerable problem. Not only did she lack a car, but she also never obtained a driver's license.

On the day of the therapist appointment, she was up before noon. Despite the early start, she moved through her morning in a fog, her mind preoccupied with the plans she had set in motion. My two-year-old brother was a whirlwind of energy, running back and forth across the kitchen, his shrieking sounds piercing through the haze of her thoughts.

She sat at the kitchen table, stirring her instant coffee absentmindedly as she watched his antics. Her gaze occasionally drifted to the calendar where she had marked the appointment date—a small, satisfied smile touched her lips as she imagined the outcome of the day's events. The sharp ring of the doorbell jolted my mother from her trance. She called out, "Come in." Before she had finished, the door had already swung open, revealing my maternal grandmother, Rebecca. My mother had asked her to come over that afternoon to watch my brother while she attended my appointment.

Rebecca was unlike my mother. She moved with a natural grace and offered a comforting presence, her smile a beacon of warmth.

In those brief moments when Rebecca was with us, it felt as though the world slowed down, offering a glimpse of what life could be like if tenderness and care were the norm rather than the exception. Rebecca lived on Avenue J in Brooklyn, a trip of up to two hours on public transportation from us. From the bus stop, she then faced a one-mile walk to our doorstep.

Despite the journey, she approached each visit with dedication. She would load up a shopping bag with thoughtful gifts and a large container of her renowned homemade chicken noodle soup—a comforting staple she knew would be appreciated in my mother's often tumultuous household. Simmered to perfection and packed with care, the soup was more than a meal; it was a symbol of Rebecca's love and concern.

My brother, eager for attention, reached up to her with a bright smile. Rebecca responded with affection, gently placing both hands on either side of his face and leaning down to meet his gaze. After sharing a tender moment with her grandson, Rebecca turned to my mother, enveloping her in a heartfelt hug. The embrace was filled with a depth of understanding that transcended words. My mother's usual tension seemed to momentarily soften as she held her mother close, and Rebecca could sense that something was amiss.

They sat at the kitchen table, with the two-year-old perched comfortably on Rebecca's lap as she wondered what was on Helen's mind. The warmth of the soup and the presence of the gifts added a touch of normalcy to the scene, yet tension lingered in the air. My mother, normally so open with Rebecca, now seemed hesitant. She avoided eye contact, her gaze shifting away as Rebecca began to ask about the day's plans.

Though my mother had not yet mentioned anything about a therapist appointment or her plans regarding me, Rebecca's intuition told her that something significant was brewing.

My mother's eyes darted to the clock on the kitchen wall. She turned to Rebecca, her voice carrying a hint of impatience as she said,

“The bus should be pulling up any minute now.” My mother led the way to the bay window in the living room, which offered a clear view of the street below. Rebecca followed, her curiosity piqued by the subtle shift in my mother’s demeanor..

Within minutes, a yellow school bus rumbled past the house and pulled up at the corner. My mother’s gaze was fixed on the scene. I, along with a few other neighborhood kids, disembarked and began walking toward the house. My casual stride towards the house seemed to intensify my mother’s focus, and Rebecca felt a growing unease.

I opened the front door and stepped into the entrance foyer, my face flushed from the crisp air. I moved with a familiar ease, walking over to the steps where I plopped down, resting my notebook beside me. I pulled off my sneakers without bothering to untie the laces before tossing them in the air. They sailed across the tile floor, landing with a series of comical thuds and imaginary explosions, a game only I seemed to fully appreciate.

As I settled into my spot, I heard my grandmother’s voice calling “Mitchel!” My head snapped up, my expression shifting from carefree to startled. I looked up, my eyes widening as I recognized the familiar voice. “Grammy!” I shouted in delighted surprise. I scrambled up the stairs, eagerly. We embraced in a heartfelt hug. I squeezed my grandmother tightly; she responded with a loving kiss on the top of my head, her affection evident.

Chapter 5

The Calm Before the Storm

"Don't forget we have a doctor's appointment later. We're just waiting for your father to get home," my mother said, her tone carrying an edge of impatience. I barely acknowledged her words. I walked around her with a slight shrug and made my way to my room. Once inside, I closed the door behind me, creating a small sanctuary.

The mention of the doctor's appointment barely registered with me. It seemed distant and irrelevant.

I plopped down into my desk chair, the familiar creak beneath me a comforting sound. As I glanced around my room, I felt a sense of calm wash over me. Instinctively, I reached for my desk drawer and pulled it open. My fingers found a partially completed color by number picture, a cherished project that had become my retreat. With a gentle touch, I removed the picture and set it on the desk, the sight of it already easing my mind. I reached for my set of colored pencils, each one a small beacon of calm. I selected my colors and began to work on the picture.

I heard Rebecca tell my mother she needed to get dressed. My mother retreated to the bathroom to begin her ritual of applying makeup, a process she had perfected over the years. Her style was rooted in the glamorous looks of the 1950s, inspired by the actresses she admired on late-night television.

As the 1970s approached, however, her retro style seemed increasingly out of place. My mother's efforts extended beyond makeup. She carefully attached a wig to her thinning brown hair, securing it with bobby pins.

Her natural complexion was pale, a feature she accentuated with a white powder foundation. The powder cast a ghostly pallor over her skin, creating a striking contrast to the vibrant hues of her makeup. The bold red lipstick, heavy eyeliner, and blush seemed out of place against her otherwise washed-out face, making her look like a character from another time, caught between theatrical elegance and harsh reality.

My father opened the front door, the familiar creak signaling his arrival. As he reached the top step, my mother's voice cut through the quiet. "Are you going to be ready to leave for the doctor soon?" she asked, her tone brisk and expectant. "Yeah, just give me a little while," he replied, his voice carrying a hint of fatigue.

Standing before the bathroom mirror, my father grappled with the decision that loomed over him. The reason for taking their son to a therapist was still not entirely clear to him, despite the discussions and his wife's insistence. My father recalled the meeting with my teacher. He remembered the discussion about my behavioral issues—an assessment that had seemed so clinical and detached at the time. He pondered the teacher's concerns, trying to reconcile them with his own experiences. "Don’t most young kids have issues?"- he thought, frustration tinged with denial. It seemed to my father that children, by their very nature, were prone to missteps of unpredictability. Surely, these were just typical growing pains, not signs of something more serious. In the quiet of the bathroom, my father wrestled with the nagging feeling that perhaps they were overreacting. Was it really necessary to send my son to a therapist? The mirror offered no answers, only the reflection of a man caught between parental concern and the looming specter of a decision he was not entirely convinced was right.

"Alright, I’m ready to go,"- my father announced, his voice carrying a note of resignation. My mother opened the door to my room. “Here, put this on,” she said, tossing me my jacket with a hint of disgust.

I caught the jacket with my free hand, the pencils still gripped tightly in the other. I quickly returned my drawing to the desk drawer. As I slipped on the jacket, I felt disoriented by the sudden flurry of activity. I glanced over at my grandmother, who stood quietly just outside my room. Her expression was one of concern and resignation, a silent witness to the unfolding events.

With a nod to Rebecca, I followed my mother and father downstairs. The house, usually so filled with tension, now seemed a distant backdrop to the appointment that lay ahead.

I settled into the back seat of the car, fixating on the back of my mother's head as we drove. I noticed the numerous bobby pins securing her wig, each one a reminder of her obsession with appearances. My mother stared out of the passenger window. Her pale reflection reminded me of ghostly comic book characters. The thirty-minute drive felt interminable. The silence in the car was punctuated only by the steady hum of the engine, amplifying my growing sense of dread.

My father scanned for a parking spot near the therapist's office. My mother took the opportunity to remove a small mirror from her handbag. She carefully checked her hair and makeup, her smile reflecting a sense of satisfaction and finality. As my father maneuvered the car into a space, she spun around abruptly, "Let's go, Mitchel," she barked, her tone leaving no room for hesitation. We walked to the therapist's office in silence, maintaining a distance from one another. The receptionist greeted us warmly, reaching out to shake my father's hand.

"Hi, Mr. Rosen," she said. "The doctor will be with you soon. Please, have a seat." My parents and I sat together in the waiting area simply because there were only four chairs available. The doctor emerged and introduced himself. As I stepped into the examination room, he turned back to my parents, reminding them that the examination would take about an hour.

I entered the exam room feeling apprehensive. The room had soft lighting and comfortable furniture. The doctor gestured for me to take a seat. I looked around, trying to make sense of the situation while he spoke gently. The minutes ticked by slowly. My confusion grew as I surveyed the small, unadorned space. Instead of the familiar medical instruments and equipment, the room featured just a small table with a couple of chairs. The doctor, seated at the table, gestured for me to sit across from him. I wondered what kind of doctor this could be. There were no medical devices like stethoscopes or scales, no cotton balls or wooden sticks typically associated with physical exams. The absence of these items made me question the nature of this appointment and whether it was the usual kind of check-up I was used to.

My curiosity intensified as he wheeled a square box out of a closet. The box was connected to a jumble of wires, creating a maze of tangled cables that snaked around the room. He carefully placed a helmet on my head, attaching wires and electrodes to various points. The setup was elaborate; the helmet felt strange, and the wires seemed to pulse slightly, adding to my unease.

He explained that the equipment was used to measure brain activity and to understand how I was feeling. Although I didn't fully grasp the technical details, I was reassured by his calm demeanor. The process would involve a series of tests and observations, and he made it clear that there was nothing to worry about.

I focused on small details in the room—the way the light played on surfaces, the hum of the machine. Despite my nervousness, I found some comfort in the routine of the tests. The session lasted for an hour, with the doctor periodically checking the readings and asking me questions.

"Okay, Mitchel, you did great! We're all done," he said with a reassuring smile. "Now, you're going to switch places with your parents." He guided me to the waiting room and signaled to my parents to follow him. I remained alone in the waiting room, fixating on the wall clock.

I wondered what the doctor and my parents were discussing and hoped that whatever was happening would lead to a positive outcome. In the examination room, the doctor smiled at my parents. "I have some rather good news," he began. "After a thorough examination, I'm pleased to inform you that your son does not meet the criteria for any specific mental health disorders, such as depression, anxiety, or bipolar disorder," he said.

"He exhibits normal cognitive functioning, including memory, attention, and problem-solving abilities. Furthermore, there are no significant abnormalities in his mood, behavior, or thought processes that would suggest a mental health issue."

My father nodded affirmatively to indicate that he understood what was being said. My mother's facial expressions were changing rapidly. Initially, she was confused and surprised, then disappointed. "I also conducted a Stanford-Binet IQ test. Your son's score was above average, the doctor added.

You're wrong, you're wrong! my mother shouted, glaring, and balling her hands into fists. What about his teacher, was she making it up! my mother screamed. "I'm sorry Mrs. Rosen, but the Stanford-Binet IQ tests are overseen by professional organizations and psychometricians," he replied. "I don't care! she responded. The doctor glanced over at my father who didn't appear to be surprised by her behavior. "Mr. Rosen, would you mind if I just speak with your wife for a moment?" the doctor asked. Without hesitation, my father returned to the waiting room.

After about thirty minutes of speaking with my mother the doctor thanked her for her time and escorted her to the waiting room. My father and I rose to go. "Mr. Rosen, could I just have a minute with you," the doctor asked. My father walked back and stepped inside his office. Mr. Rosen, has your wife ever had a psychiatric evaluation before? the doctor asked. "She's been like this for years, Doc. I don't know what to do," my father replied, his voice tinged with frustration and concern. The doctor nodded, his expression thoughtful. "From the brief interaction I've had with her this evening, I would say she appears to be suffering from a major depressive disorder. There are also signs of a potential mental health disorder that needs further evaluation."

He paused to ensure that my father understood. "I recommend having her evaluated by a mental health professional to develop an appropriate treatment plan. This may involve psychotherapy, medication, or a combination of both." "Thank you, Doctor," my father said with gratitude. We left in silence, my mother purposefully avoiding the receptionist's warm smile and wave. My father and I, on the other hand, offered a courteous smile and a nod before following my mother out.

The ride home was excruciating. My mother's face was twisted into a scowl as she stared out the window. I noticed her clenched fists and the way she seemed to mutter to herself.

I was prepared for the brewing storm, and kept my gaze fixed on my lap, too afraid to make eye contact. In our driveway, my father put the car in park, silently waiting for my mother to make the first move.

I watched as she stormed to the front door. Over time, both my father and I had learned to give her space, recognizing that stepping back was the best way to avoid setting off her explosive temper.

My father noticed Rebecca watching from the upstairs bay window. My mother marched up the stairs, bypassing her on the landing. Rebecca recognized that stormy expression on my mother's face; she was deeply concerned about what might happen next.

My father entered the house just as my mother slammed the bathroom door shut. "What happened?" Rebecca asked. My father could only shrug and reply, "I don't know what happened." He offered a strained smile before walking past her and heading to the bedroom. I trudged up the stairs, my head bowed as I tried to make sense of the turmoil I had just witnessed. On the verge of tears, I looked up and saw my grandmother. "Grammy!" I shouted, my voice breaking. With renewed energy, I raced up the stairs and extended my arms toward Rebecca. We embraced tightly, finding comfort in each other's presence amid the chaos.

Chapter 6

The Suitcase

A few days later, my mother began to re-evaluate her plan. The doctor's diagnosis had been a blow; his report indicated I had no abnormalities and a high IQ. "How can I make this work?" she wondered.

My mother reflected on recent events where I had gotten into trouble, trying to piece together my behavior. One incident stood out vividly in her mind: about a month ago, at the bus stop, I and another boy were having a wild time. We were swinging our books around by the rubber straps that were popular in the 1960s—straps that wrapped around the books and were secured with metal hooks, making them easier to carry. We laughed as we swung our books higher and higher. Suddenly, the rubber strap holding my books snapped. The books flew through the air, and the metal hook from the strap struck a little girl in the face.

Although the incident had clearly been an accident, I was suspended from school for a few days. My mother recalled the episode and decided to use it. Her plan was back in motion, but it needed a new approach. Over the following days, she began fabricating stories about my behavior. Each evening, when my father came home, she would tell him that I was out of control and that she could no longer handle me.

I sensed something was off about my mother's recent behavior. To avoid her unwarranted punishments, I began locking myself in my room as soon as I got home from school. With my money running low, I could no longer afford to buy sandwiches, leaving me increasingly worried about how to manage my situation. My father had his own escape: on weekends, he would retreat to the basement to paint. I occasionally joined him, watching my father paint for hours. The process was not only relaxing but also sparked my interest in art.

In the following weeks, my mother kept persuading my father that I had problematic behavior that needed to be addressed. He was puzzled, as he had never observed such behavior from me. Nonetheless, he realized that to keep the peace and manage the situation, he had to comply with her request. Her plan was to have me re-evaluated. The appointment was set for Monday, September 12, 1966. My father planned to take the day off for another evaluation. A couple of days beforehand, I was informed that I wouldn't be going to school that day. I was thrilled at the prospect of a day off, thinking it sounded like a nice break.

On the morning of September 12, I was puzzled to see my father at home and even more surprised that my mother was awake before noon. "This must be that no-school day," I thought. My mother seemed unusually stressed; she hadn't done her hair and was still in her pajamas. Without a word, she brushed past me in the hallway and entered my room, carrying a small suitcase.

I was disoriented by the commotion around me, but I reminded myself that I had the day off from school. My father's voice called out, "Come on, Mitchel, let's go!" He was heading down the stairs with the small suitcase in hand. I watched as he tossed the suitcase into the back seat of the car. I jumped into the passenger seat realizing that my mother wouldn't be joining us after all. The streets of the neighborhood gave way to the broader expanse of Manhattan, and I gazed out of the window, taking in the changing scenery.

As we crossed into Manhattan, a strange vibe settled over the car. The towering skyscrapers and bustling streets seemed to amplify the silence within the vehicle. My eyes followed the cityscape, but my mind was preoccupied with the unsettling shift in my father's demeanor. I sensed something was amiss.

My father slowed the car as he began the search for a parking space along Madison Avenue. I gazed at the high-rise buildings that seemed to stretch endlessly towards the sky. I had no clear idea where we were headed or why we had come to Manhattan in the first place. The sense of adventure was overshadowed by apprehension.

We exited the car, my father grabbed the suitcase from the back seat. I followed as we walked past several buildings. Up ahead, my attention was drawn to a building that stood out from the rest. It had a distinctive entrance, marked by an array of doors through which a steady stream of people passed. What struck me as odd was the large number of people wearing long white jackets. They moved with purpose, their attire making them seem like part of a coordinated team.

As we approached the entrance, my eyes landed on a large sign in the foyer that read, “Mount Sinai Hospital.” The realization hit me like a jolt—I was at a hospital. The sudden clarity of the situation brought a surge of concern. My mind raced as I tried to piece together what might be happening. My father, now entering through the doors, seemed focused and purposeful. I followed, my steps hesitant. I wondered why we were there and what it meant for our day. Is Dad sick? Why are we here?

We stepped into the elevator. I stood beside a man clad in a long white coat, his expression distant.

The clinical, impersonal atmosphere of the elevator only heightened my unease. When the elevator doors finally slid open, I looked up at my father, seeking some reassurance. He met my gaze and gave a slight nod, conveying both determination and a sense of urgency. It was a silent signal that we were moving forward, even as my mind struggled to catch up with the situation.

Exiting the elevator we were immediately confronted with a large glass partition. It looked like a barrier, one that separated us from whatever awaited beyond and added to my sense of disorientation. My heart pounded as we approached the counter. The woman behind the counter looked up and greeted us with a warm smile. She wore a crisp white collared shirt and a small white triangular hat perched neatly on her head. The contrast between her composed appearance and the chaotic sounds emanating from beyond the partition was striking.

The moment she slid open a small window in the glass, the muffled sounds of screaming children and the buzz of activity spilled out into the otherwise quiet hallway. The noise was loud and jarring. The woman leaned forward, straining to hear my father's voice over the clamor. The situation seemed increasingly surreal. I couldn't help but feel a pang of worry—what kind of place were we entering?

I watched the interaction, trying to decipher the purpose of our visit and the nature of the place we had entered. "I'm here to drop my son off," my father stated, his voice formal. The woman glanced down at her log, "What's the last name?" she asked, "Rosen," my father replied, his tone clipped. At that moment, time froze for me. A wave of anxiety surged through me, overwhelming my senses. The revelation of my last name being called out, the formality of the situation, and the clinical environment of the hospital suddenly felt very real. My heart raced, my mind swirling with confusion and fear. Why was I being taken to the hospital? What was happening?

The woman behind the counter glanced at me with a look of gentle reassurance, then walked around to a side door. Another woman, who stood waiting beside her, extended her hand towards me and led me further into the hospital. I noticed my suitcase standing beside her. The moment my hand grasped hers, I heard the faint, definitive sound of the door closing behind me. I turned to look back through the glass partition, my eyes searching for my father.

Without a word, my father had already left, making his way back to the elevator. My heart sank as I watched my father leave. The sense of abandonment and uncertainty was crushing.

Chapter 7

The Sound of Silence

As the woman guided me down the hospital corridor, the harsh screams of children in pain grew more pronounced. The woman remained composed, occasionally glancing back at me with a reassuring smile, but the relentless cries of the children drowned out her attempts at comfort. As we walked, I found it increasingly difficult to process my surroundings. The corridor seemed to stretch on endlessly, its clinical, fluorescent lighting casting an impersonal glow over everything. The noise from the other side of the walls felt almost oppressive, a constant reminder of the distressing situation unfolding around me.

The woman finally led me to a doorway, which she opened with a gentle push. I stepped through, hoping for some respite from the overwhelming noise. With the door closed, the sound of the children's cries muffled, but the tension remained. "This is your room," she announced, as she placed my suitcase alongside the bed. She hesitated for a moment before exiting. The door clicked shut behind her, leaving me behind in the silence of the room. The room itself was modest, with a single bed covered in plain white linens. A small grate-covered window was set into one wall, offering a view of the street below.

The street noise was faint, but the occasional honk or murmur from outside served as a reminder of the world beyond the confines of this small space. I sat on the edge of the bed, feeling the weight of the day's events pressing down on me. My hands moved to cover my eyes, a futile gesture of hope that when I opened them again, I'd be somewhere else—somewhere familiar and comforting, far from the confusion and anxiety of the hospital. But when I finally moved my hands away, the room remained unchanged, the reality of my circumstances still very much present. I took a deep breath, trying to steady myself. The quiet of the room did nothing to soothe my troubled mind; it only made the solitude more apparent. The bed felt like an island in a sea of uncertainty. I was alone.

As I looked around the room, my gaze landed on the suitcase beside my bed. It was a tangible connection to my father, and its presence was both a comfort and a reminder of the abrupt separation. I knew I had to find a way to cope with the situation, to navigate this new reality with whatever courage I could muster. But for now, I sat on the bed, overwhelmed by the day's events and the unsettling quiet of the room.

Suddenly, the room was filled with the soft strains of music emanating from the ceiling speakers. The unexpected sound broke the silence, and after a moment of disorientation, my curiosity pulled me towards the grated window.

I stood there, staring down at the street below. Autumn was upon us as people walked freely, enjoying the day, their laughter and chatter drifting up to where I stood. Thc sight of their carefree existence heightened my sense of isolation.

I felt as though I were a spectator, watching a world that was both familiar and impossibly distant. The music playing overhead was "The Sound of Silence" by Simon and Garfunkel, a song that resonated deeply with my mood. As the song wove its way through the room, its melancholy tones created a backdrop to my growing sense of despair. "Hello darkness, my old friend."

Suddenly, there was a knock on the door, and before I could react, it swung open. A woman with a warm smile stepped in. "Hello, Mitchel," she said, extending her hand. "My name is Janet. I'll be taking care of you while you're here." She had an air of calm confidence, "Let's take a walk. I'd like to introduce you to Dr. Thomas, who will be your therapist."

As Janet escorted me down the hall, the stark reality of the place began to sink in. We passed a child sitting on the floor, his small frame slumped against the wall as he repeatedly banged his head against the concrete. His expression was blank, his actions rhythmic and relentless. A few feet away, another boy was thrashing and shouting, his cries echoing through the corridor as two orderlies struggled to restrain him.

"Okay, here we are," Janet said, opening a door and motioning for me to enter. Dr. Thomas looked up from his work, his smile warm but tinged with concern. He rose and approached me. He was a short, heavyset man with a balding head and flushed cheeks. He clasped his hands in front of him and asked gently, “Do you have any questions?” Overwhelmed by frustration and anxiety, I couldn’t hold back my tears any longer. I began to sob uncontrollably, my voice trembling as I repeated, “Why am I here? Why am I here?” Dr. Thomas's expression softened. “This is just for an evaluation, that’s all.” The words barely registered through my distress.

I didn’t fully understand what an evaluation meant, but the uncertainty only deepened my worry about what lay ahead. As time went by, I slowly grew accustomed to the daily routines. Mornings began with the piercing screams of the boy in the neighboring room—his outbursts lasted for about five minutes each day. Other children needed to be physically restrained, while some wandered around in a dazed state. Day after day, I walked the halls, listening to the cacophony of cries, witnessing outbursts of anger, and observing peculiar behaviors. Each day stretched endlessly, marked by the relentless noise and isolation. Despite the ward being filled with children, I felt profoundly alone. From my window, I saw the comfortable days of autumn give way to the cool, crisp days of the approaching winter.

Just when I started to believe that my family had forgotten about me, Janet popped her head into my room. “Mitchel, you’re going home tomorrow!” she announced, her voice brimming with excitement. In an instant, the weight of depression lifted from my shoulders. I felt a surge of exhilaration, as if I’d been injected with a burst of superpowers. That afternoon, I walked the halls with a newfound energy, my steps quicker and a smile spreading across my face. Finally, the long-awaited day had arrived! I couldn't stop thinking about everything I'd missed—my friends from school, my room, the familiar routines. Curiously, my thoughts did not linger on my mother.

The day before I was set to leave, the doctor assigned to my case called and spoke with my mother. He reviewed the results of my thirty-day evaluation with her. "The evaluation didn't reveal any conclusive results," he explained. "However, your son scored above average on our Stanford-Binet IQ test." My mother had anticipated the results based on the initial evaluation, but ultimately, it didn't seem to matter. It was done, and the final outcome was inescapable.

Chapter 8

Columbus Day

I woke up the next morning with a smile that felt as though it would never fade. Janet slowly opened my door, her smile mirroring my own. “Are you excited, Mitchel?” she asked as she watched me skip from the bed to the door. “Is my dad here?” I asked, my smile widening. “He should be here soon,” she replied.

Not knowing quite what to do with myself, I wandered the halls with a nervous energy, occasionally glancing toward the front, where the nurses' station was located. It seemed quieter than usual. The usual bustle of nurses walking briskly down the corridors, was absent. I sat there, waiting, when I overheard one nurse talking to another. "Enjoy Columbus Day!" she said.

I remembered learning about Christopher Columbus in school—how he sailed across the ocean in search of new lands, how he accidentally stumbled upon what would become America. It dawned on me that today was a holiday, a day off for many. But for those of us here, life continued, indifferent to the calendar.

I waited patiently in my room. I smiled, knowing that shortly I would be free of this nightmare. I listened to the music from the speakers above: The Four Tops’ new single, “Standing in the Shadows of Love." The song spoke of getting ready for heartache. The lyrics spoke to my own feelings—anxiety, anticipation, the sense that something was shifting but I wasn't quite sure how.

I leaned against the metal grate which covered the window, trying to lose myself in the music. Suddenly a nurse's voice cut through my thoughts. "Your father's here!" she announced. Time seemed to slow down for a moment. The words hung in the air, heavy with meaning. My father's here. The phrase carried a weight that the nurse couldn't have understood. My heart raced as I processed what this meant.

I turned slowly from the window, emotions washing over me—relief, apprehension, hope. My suitcase was packed and waiting up front, a testament to my readiness to leave. It had been sitting there, like a promise of escape, of returning to something familiar, something safe. I hurried down the hall, my feet barely touching the floor as I ran in my father's direction. I could see him standing at the nurses' station, tall and steady, but as I got closer, a sinking feeling started to replace the excitement that had fueled my steps.

At first, I thought it was just my imagination, that the distance between us was playing tricks on my mind. But as I neared, the truth became undeniable. The vibe, the energy I had expected to feel from him, wasn't there. His posture was stiff, his face set in a neutral expression that offered none of the warmth I had hoped for. My heart, which had been racing with anticipation, began to falter. I kept moving forward, even as a part of me wanted to turn around and retreat back down the hall, to the room where everything was still familiar. His failure to make eye contact cut deeper than any words could have. It was as if I didn't exist in that moment, as if being here was just another task for him to complete.

I felt crushed. Doubts began to crowd my mind, whispering that maybe I had been foolish to hope for anything more. But then I reminded myself of something I had learned long ago—my father was not very good in the communication department. He had never been one for big displays of emotion or words of comfort. This was just how he was.

I needed to give him a chance, even if it was hard. I stepped up beside him, standing close enough to feel the solidity of his presence but careful not to expect too much. He was focused on signing documents the nurse handed him. I waved goodbye, a half-hearted gesture that felt more like a formality than a farewell. My father held the door for me, his face still unreadable. We walked to the elevator in silence. Once inside, I pressed the button for the lobby. I felt a quiet sense of accomplishment, as if I had earned that small but significant moment of control.

We stood in the small, sterile space, just the two of us. I stole a glance at him, hoping to catch his eye, to find some sign of what he was feeling. But his gaze remained fixed ahead, avoiding mine. Something was definitely going on, but I couldn't figure out what.

We stepped outside. My father's gray Ford Fairlane was parked a few steps away, its chrome trim gleaming dully in the morning light. It was the same car we'd had for years, a reliable but unremarkable presence in our lives, much like my father.

I jumped into the passenger seat and let my imagination take over. In my mind's eye, the gray Ford Fairlane transformed into the sleek, black Batmobile, its powerful engine roaring to life. I could almost hear the whine of the turbines and feel the vibration of the engine beneath me. I was no longer just a kid in an old car—I was Robin, ready to race through the streets of Gotham City alongside Batman, ready for whatever adventure awaited us.

I glanced over at my father, and for a second, I saw him differently. He wasn't just my dad anymore; he was Batman, the stoic hero who always had a plan, even if he kept it to himself. I imagined him pressing a secret button on the dashboard, igniting the Batmobile's afterburners as fire shot out of the tailpipes.

The car would leap forward, speeding off to save the day, just like in the TV show. But as quickly as the fantasy appeared, it faded. The reality of the situation settled back in, and I was just a boy sitting next to his father, waiting for the engine to start.

Yet, even as I settled back into the seat, I held onto a tiny piece of that fantasy. It was a comforting thought—that maybe, just maybe, there was a part of my father that was like Batman: quiet, reserved, but always there to protect me when I needed him most. I couldn't be sure, but for now, that small hope was enough.

I started daydreaming about returning home to my friends and my room. I gave up trying to get my father's attention, so I just turned in my seat and pressed my face up against the passenger window glass.

As we drove, I became more confused. I felt that after thirty minutes of driving things would start to look familiar. Instead, we were driving places I've never seen before? I turned and looked at my father who seemed to have tears in his eye's? I continued to stare until he pulled the car to the curb. When he turned to face me I noticed that his face was red, his eyes glazed, and his lips dry. You're not going home! He said, sounding remorseful. Tears instantly cascaded down my face. I felt my chest tighten, and my stomach twist into knots. I completely shut down, not listening to anything my father was saying! It just didn't matter. I was not going home!

We continued to drive, and I noticed my father's hand briefly leave the steering wheel, and wipe the tears from his eyes. It was a quick, almost furtive gesture, but it didn't escape my notice. My father, who rarely showed emotion, was crying. The sight stirred something deep inside me, a mixture of confusion, concern, and a longing to understand what was going on in his mind. But the words to ask him what was wrong never came. I stayed silent, my gaze shifting to the world outside the car window.

The neighborhood we were driving through was far from familiar. The houses looked different—older, worn down, their facades cracked and faded. The streets seemed narrower, hemmed in by buildings that loomed closer than I was used to. I caught glimpses of people lying on the sidewalks, their bodies twisted in uncomfortable positions, as if they had simply collapsed there. Their faces were gaunt, their clothes ragged, and their presence added a layer of sadness to the already bleak surroundings. Occasionally, shouts and screams pierced the air, drawing my attention to small groups of people drinking beer while arguing, their voices carrying over the roar of the city. Fights broke out in the open, fists flying, while others watched with disinterest or joined in. The sight of it all made my stomach churn.

Steel trash cans, dented and scuffed, rolled into the street, driven by gusts of wind or the careless kicks of passersby.

Cars, including ours, maneuvered around them, their drivers honking impatiently as they swerved to avoid the obstacles. The clanging sound of metal on asphalt echoed in my ears, adding to the dissonance of the scene.

As we continued through the unfamiliar streets, I found myself clutching the edge of my seat, wishing for the comfort of home, for something familiar to hold onto. But that comfort felt far away, just as distant as the answers I wanted from my father. Twenty minutes later, after what felt like an eternity of winding through unfamiliar streets, we finally turned onto Boerum Street in Williamsburg, Brooklyn. The neighborhood had a different feel—quieter, but with an underlying tension that made me uneasy.

The buildings here were old, their brick facades weathered. As we pulled up in front of one such building, I noticed the faded numbers “130” etched into the brick beside the entrance. The building itself had an imposing presence. Five slate steps, chipped and uneven from years of use, led up to a set of heavy wooden doors. These were framed by two massive white columns, their paint peeling in places, supporting a concrete overhang. The overhang cast a long shadow over the entrance, giving the place an air of both grandeur and foreboding.

We sat in the car, neither of us making a move to get out. My father gripped the steering wheel tightly. He was still, except for the occasional deep breath, as if he was trying to gather the strength to face whatever lay ahead. I could see the tension in his jaw, the way his eyes were fixed on the building in front of us, yet seemed to look past it, as if searching for something far beyond what was visible.

I followed his gaze and let my eyes drift up to the building. That’s when I noticed the name “Childville” carved into the face of the concrete overhang above the door. The word sent a chill through me, its meaning sinking in slowly, like cold water seeping through cracks.

Childville. The name was simple, almost benign, but there was something about it that made my heart beat faster, my palms started to sweat. It was as if the building itself was trying to tell me something,

something I wasn't ready to hear. The silence between my father and me grew heavier, filled with all the unspoken fears and questions that neither of us dared to voice.

I wanted to ask my father why we were here, what this place was, but the words caught in my throat. I wasn't sure I wanted to know the answer. He finally let out a long, shaky breath and released his grip on the steering wheel. He wiped his eyes again, this time more deliberately, and turned to look at me. His face was tired, lined with worry, but there was a resolve in his expression that hadn't been there before. I knew then that whatever was about to happen, it was something he had been dreading for a long time.

Before we exited the car, my father erupted, "There was nothing I could do!" His voice was charged with frustration as he placed the blame for the outcome squarely on my mother. As he continued to plead his case, I found my hearing beginning to shut down, overwhelmed by his insistence. While I agreed that the decision had been primarily my mother's idea, my father's lack of objection spoke volumes about his own role in the situation. Without a word, I reached for the door handle and left the car. My father walked alongside me as we approached the slate steps. The world outside the car felt distant, as if we were stepping into a different reality. The heavy doors of Childville loomed ahead, and with every step I took toward them, I felt a little more of my childhood slipping away.

Just as we reached the top, the door swung open. A white man in his thirties appeared. He had shoulder-length brown curly hair that framed his face, and a beard that gave him a rugged; yet approachable look. His eyes were kind, but there was a seriousness about him that made me nervous. He was clearly a hippie of the sixties.

"Hi, I'm Mr. Scott," he said. "Are you Mr. Rosen?" My father nodded. "I'm your son's counselor," Mr. Scott continued, his gaze shifting to me for the first time. There was something in his eyes, a mixture of understanding and responsibility, that made me feel small, like a child about to be handed over to someone else's care.

The introduction was brief, almost perfunctory. My father didn't say much—just a few words exchanged between two men who both seemed to know that this moment was bigger than anything they could express. After a few seconds of silence, my father handed Mr. Scott my suitcase. I felt like a stray dog being passed from one home to another, uncertain if this new place would offer any more comfort or warmth than the last.

I wanted to cling to my father, to ask him to take me back, to tell him this was a mistake, but the words wouldn't come.

Instead, I stood there, silent and still, as Mr. Scott placed a firm but gentle hand on my shoulder, guiding me away from the man who I thought was my protector. My father turned and walked back to the car, each step taking him further away from me, just like at the hospital thirty days ago. It was an echo of that earlier day, when I had watched him leave me behind in a place that felt foreign and frightening. I felt sadness and resignation wash over me, a heavy tide pulling me under.

I watched my father until he was no longer visible. With a final glance back, I turned to face Mr. Scott and the world of Childville. The door closed behind me with a definitive thud.

Little did I know, Childville would eventually haunt me for the rest of my life. As I crossed the threshold of the heavy door and entered the dimly lit interior, I had no way of comprehending the depth of the imprint it would leave on my soul.

It was Columbus Day, 1966, a holiday this eight-year-old had barely noticed until now. But as I walked beside Mr. Scott, I knew this day would be carved in my memory forever. It wasn't just another day off from school; it was the day my life changed.

Chapter 9

Welcome to Childville

Childville was a juvenile facility built to house children who were deemed problematic or unwanted. It wasn't designed to heal or rehabilitate; it served as a temporary refuge for those who had been labeled too difficult, too broken, or simply discarded. Much like stray animals awaiting adoption, these children were left there to wait for a chance at a new beginning, their future's uncertain and their hopes fragile.

It was a state-run home where children like me were left to navigate their own struggles in an environment of neglect and minimal support. My parents decided to abandon me to this institution, seeking an escape from their own issues and insecurities. The facility was a last resort, a place for those who had nowhere else to turn, and its very existence spoke volumes about the societal attitudes towards children who were deemed problematic.

The building was a three-story brownstone. In the rear was a small, cement-covered yard, a stark and unwelcoming space enclosed by a ten-foot-high chain-link fence. The fence was not merely a boundary; it was a statement, a barrier designed to keep the outside world from intruding. Vertical privacy slats were attached to the fence, ensuring that any interaction with the surrounding community was minimal.

The children inside were often the products of broken homes, abusive parents, or circumstances that had left them without a family member to care for them. The shared experiences of loss, neglect, and trauma created an atmosphere of collective pain and confusion. The staff, often undertrained and overwhelmed, struggled to provide any meaningful support or guidance, leaving the children to fend for themselves in an environment that was anything but nurturing. The small yard, with its unforgiving fence, was a place where many of us spent our time, staring out at a world that felt forever out of reach. The fence symbolized the emotional and psychological barriers we faced—both the barriers we built around ourselves and those imposed on us by the institution. In this setting, the sense of isolation was profound.

The children who inhabited Childville were bound together not by friendship or camaraderie but by a shared sense of abandonment and displacement. Each day was a struggle to find some sense of stability or hope amid the harsh realities of life within those walls. The past was never far away, and the future seemed like a distant, unreachable dream. Childville was situated in a deeply impoverished section of Williamsburg, an area that was as neglected as the children it housed.

The neighborhood surrounding the facility was a stark contrast to the world of opportunity and security that many children might have dreamt of. It was a place of desperation and survival.

That first day, Mr. Scott walked me down the first-floor hallway to the lunchroom. It was a utilitarian space, filled with eight round tables and chairs, the linoleum floor beneath them worn and scuffed. The room connected to the kitchen, a small, functional area that churned out basic meals for the children. The smell of overcooked vegetables and a hint of disinfectant hung in the air.

We proceeded up a flight of stairs. As we climbed, my gaze was drawn to Mr. Scott's footwear, which was unlike anything I had ever seen before. His foot rested on a flat, leather sole held in place by intricately looping leather straps. They were sandals, something I had seen in *Ben-Hur*, —a film set in ancient Rome, starring Charlton Heston.

They were also a fashion choice for hippies in the 1960s, a symbol of their desire to reconnect with simpler, more natural ways of life. This blend of historical and contemporary references contrasted with the harshness of the facility.

It was a reminder that even in a place like this, there were fragments of the outside world trying to find their way in.

Mr. Scott informed me that the girls' bunks were on the second floor, while the third floor was the "boys'" area. The stairs opened up into a large common room, a sprawling space that seemed to serve as the heart of the "boys'" section.

It was sparsely furnished with a few worn-out sofas and mismatched chairs, arranged haphazardly around a central table that held a large black and white television set. From this central room, two hallways branched off, narrow and dimly lit, with bare walls. These led to the boy's bunks, each of which featured three metal-framed beds and a shared dresser. The metal frames were cold and unyielding. The beds creaked and groaned with every movement, the springs protesting against the thin, three-inch-thick mattresses. Getting used to the constant noise of popping springs became an unwelcome part of my routine.

When I entered the room assigned to me, the reality of our living conditions hit hard. Two of the beds were neatly made, their sheets smoothed out with a care that seemed out of place in our sparse surroundings. My bed, however, was starkly different. It was positioned at the end of the room, its plastic mattress marred by unsightly urine stains. As the first few days at Childville passed, I began to understand the structure and daily routines of the facility. Mr. Scott was responsible for a group of around five boys.

His role was to oversee their daily activities, provide guidance, and address any issues that arose. This group dynamic was crucial in creating a semblance of order. Mr. Scott shared these responsibilities with a staff member named Ms. Susan, also in her mid to late thirties. Like him, she wore leather sandals. She had long, wavy brown hair that cascaded down her back, often catching the light in a way that made it seem almost golden. Her glasses, with their round lenses, lent her an air of thoughtful contemplation.

She typically wore a sundress whose flowing fabric and gentle flower patterns contrasted with the facility's starkness.

Each group of children was assigned a male and a female counselor, to create a semblance of a family structure in the facility. However, the effectiveness of this approach varied. While it provided a structure that mimicked family life, it could not fully replace the complexities and nuances of a real family environment. Despite their best efforts, the counselors were still bound by the limitations of the setting, and the challenges faced by the children often overshadowed the intended familial atmosphere.

The residents at Childville ranged in age from eight to eighteen years old, creating a diverse and often challenging mix of maturity levels and experiences. Being so young in an environment like Childville was daunting. The older boys, some nearing adulthood, carried with them a sense of authority and experience that was both intimidating and alluring to someone my age. They had already navigated the treacherous waters of adolescence within the confines of the facility, and their interactions, shaped by years of survival and adaptation, often reflected the harsh realities of their lives. The older teenagers, emboldened by their age and experience, often developed a sense of superiority over the younger, more vulnerable residents. This sense of dominance manifested itself in the form of bullying, especially toward the new arrivals who were still finding their footing in the harsh environment of the facility. The bullying wasn't just about establishing dominance—it was also a way for the older kids to cope with their own feelings of powerlessness and frustration.

In my group, there was no single race or ethnicity that held the majority. Children from all walks of life ended up together in Childville, their differences both uniting and dividing them. My group was a diverse mix of five boys: Joe, who was Black; two Spanish boys, Jose and Juan, who were often seen together; Ben, a white boy with red hair and freckles who had a quick temper; and me, an eight-year-old trying to make sense of this new reality.

The diversity within our group was a double-edged sword. On one hand, it offered a rich mix of backgrounds and experiences, but on the other, it sometimes exacerbated tensions, especially in an environment where everyone was already on edge. For me, bullying from the older kids was one of the most challenging aspects of life at Childville.

Being one of the youngest, I was an easy target, and our group didn't always provide the unity I had hoped for. Instead, it sometimes felt like everyone was just trying to survive on their own terms, and that sense of isolation made the bullying even harder to bear.

Sylvester and John, the two oldest boys in the shelter, had a room of their own. It was slightly larger than the others, a nod to their seniority and perhaps their need for a bit more privacy. The room offered a small sanctuary amid the shared spaces. It was adorned with basic paintings that were slightly better looking than the washed out gray paint on their wall. Small nightstands flanked the beds, topped with a handmade wooden lamp that held a single, functional bulb. Between the two beds lay a faded area rug. Unlike the other boys, they had no qualms about leaving their valuables on the countertops, their possessions strewn about carelessly. Their guitar and drums stood as symbols of their confidence and authority.

The understanding among the shelter's residents was clear: crossing Sylvester and John was not an option. Their reputation for ruthlessness and violence was well known, and their intimidating presence ensured that their room remained a space of both respect and fear. Their ability to maintain control and command made their room not just a refuge, but a testament to their influence within the shelter's social hierarchy.

In those early days, trust was a fragile currency. I observed closely, picking up on the subtle cues and unspoken rules that governed our interactions. I learned who to trust and who to stay clear of, as if by instinct. Some boys were quick to extend a hand of friendship, while others seemed to have an agenda of their own, their motives hidden behind practiced smiles. Navigating these relationships became a daily challenge. Trust was not easily given; it had to be earned and proven through consistent actions and shared experiences. Friendships were formed and tested in the confines of our daily lives, and each interaction was a delicate balancing act.

As I adjusted to this new world, I became adept at reading between the lines, understanding the undercurrents of tension, and finding my place in the complex web of personalities. This process of learning and adapting was a survival skill in its own right, shaping my approach to the people around me and influencing how I would ultimately cope with the confines of the shelter. Although forced to sleep on a urine-stained mattress, I somehow managed to sleep soundly through it all. My ability to sleep deeply, no matter the discomfort, was both a blessing and a defense mechanism against the constant noise and unrest of the shelter.

One morning, I woke up to an unsettling quiet. The room, usually bustling with the activity of my two roommates, was empty. The lights were glaringly bright, an unusual sight in the dimly lit rooms of our shelter. I realized that not only were the other boys missing from my room, but the entire floor seemed deserted. It turned out that during the night, the fire alarm had gone off. The entire building had been evacuated just as the fire trucks arrived with their flashing lights and blaring sirens.

Meanwhile, I slept through it all. As time passed, I couldn't shake the memory of that night when I had slept through the fire alarm. I imagined my roommates, frantic and racing past my bed to escape the flames, leaving me behind. The thought that they might have abandoned me to face the fire alone was a stark reminder: this was not a family environment; it was every man for himself.

Chapter 10

The Bathroom Break

As the days passed and I settled into the rhythms of life at the shelter, Joe quickly became my number one friend, with Ben not far behind. We were inseparable, forming a tight-knit trio that navigated the complexities of our new environment together.

With his easy going nature and quick laugh, Joe always found the bright side in even the dullest moments. Ben had a sharp wit and an adventurous streak that made every day feel like an exciting escapade. We were always up to something— sneaking into forbidden areas of the shelter, plotting elaborate pranks, or simply finding inventive ways to entertain ourselves with the limited resources we had.

One afternoon, Joe and I, fueled by mischief, crept downstairs to the kitchen. We knew the kitchen was off-limits, but the thrill of breaking the rules was too tempting to resist. The quiet hum of the refrigerator was the only sound we heard. Strange, the lights were on, casting a glare over the otherwise dimly lit room.

We exchanged glances. We were just about to turn the corner into the main area when we came face to face with Sylvester and John.

Sylvester, who was Black and stocky, with a permanent scowl on his face leaned across the counter. His presence alone commanded respect—or at least fear—from the other boys. Next to him was John, who was a lanky white guy with long blond hair that seemed perpetually untamed. He exuded an air of careless arrogance as he rummaged through the cabinets, his movements casual yet deliberate. His laid-back demeanor contrasted with Sylvester's more intense presence, but together they formed a formidable duo. They were nearing eighteen, their time at the shelter at its end. Their temporary status only added to their mystique and power within the shelter's confines.

Joe and I froze, Sylvester's eyes narrowed as he took in our presence, while John's smirk grew wider.

"Well, well, what do we have here?" Sylvester sneered. He moved in close to Joe, towering over him with a menacing glare. The eight-year-old shrank back. "This is our fuckin' kitchen," Sylvester snapped, his voice sharp and threatening. Joe turned ashen in the face of Sylvester's aggression. I watched helplessly as his hands shook visibly, a sign of the fear that gripped him. My own heart raced.

I had a sinking feeling that I was next in line for Sylvester's ire. My legs felt like lead, and I could hardly breathe as I waited for whatever would come next. John watched the scene unfold with a smirk, enjoying the power play. The kitchen felt like a trap.

"Hey John, get those two brooms over there," Sylvester barked, his voice harsh and commanding. "Yeah, that's right," John called back, his voice dripping with mockery, "Let them do the brooms."

At first, I thought they were just going to make us sweep the floor, a punishment I could handle. But as the brooms were handed over, a sinking feeling settled in my stomach. I wasn't aware that in Childville, the broom could be used as punishment.

"Okay, punks, up with the brooms!" Sylvester screamed. I watched Joe, his face flushed with effort, grip his broom with both hands at shoulder width, and extend it straight out in front of him. I mirrored his stance, trying to maintain the rigid position. "Keep those fuckin' arms straight!" Sylvester snapped. The broom felt like it was made of lead, and within fifteen seconds, my arms began to burn with an intense, searing pain. It felt as though the broom was growing heavier with every passing second, my muscles straining to keep it up. Sweat beaded on my forehead, and I could feel it trickling down my face, mingling with the tears that were welling up in my eyes. My arms started to tremble uncontrollably, and despite my best efforts, they began to drop. I tried to lift them again, but it was no use. I felt a wave of panic rise as Sylvester's face loomed inches from mine, his breath hot and taunting. "It looks like you need a good ass-kicking, cracker," Sylvester growled, his eyes narrowing with cruel satisfaction.

A sudden crashing sound echoed from the dining room, jolting Sylvester and John. Their eyes widened as they turned towards the noise. "What was that?" John muttered, his earlier bravado forgotten. Sylvester scowled and, without a word, strode towards the connecting door to investigate. As footsteps receded, Joe screamed.

"Mitch, run, run!" I dropped my broom and bolted after Joe. We flew up the stairs, burst into the bathroom and squeezed into a small stall, trying to muffle our heavy breathing and straining to hear any sounds of pursuit.

The bathroom door swung open with a force that made us jump. We held our breath, and scrambled to kneel on the toilet seat in case someone looked under the stall doors.

As we huddled there, the stall door flew open without warning. Ben, a mischievous smile playing on his lips, stood there, clearly enjoying our panicked reaction. "I knew you two went down to the kitchen," Ben said. "I heard everything with Sylvester and John." He paused letting his words sink in before adding, "I just waited for the right moment before knocking one of the dining room chairs off the table onto the floor."

The realization hit us like a jolt. Ben had orchestrated the distraction deliberately, creating a noise to cover our retreat. His smile, though friendly, was a stark contrast to the fear we had just experienced.

The bathroom, once a sanctuary of fear, now felt like a safe haven, thanks to Bens' timely intervention.

Chapter 11

The Concrete Jungle

I soon realized that Mr. Scott and Ms. Susan, the primary staff members I had come to rely on, weren't around all the time. They typically left after dinner, their departure signaling a marked shift in the shelter's atmosphere. The staff who took over the evening shift were notably less concerned about the well-being of the kids. They were often preoccupied and disengaged from their responsibilities; they showed little interest in the boys' needs or concerns, and their supervision was minimal. This created a noticeable impact on the shelter's environment.

Generally, Mr. Patrick, who was Irish, and Mr. Rodney, who was Black, covered the evening shifts.

Mr. Patrick had little trouble indulging in a few drinks before his 6 p.m. shift began. His casual approach to his responsibilities was evident in his relaxed demeanor and the lingering scent of alcohol that sometimes accompanied him. His pre-shift drinking resulted in his being hazy and his supervision less effective.

Mr. Rodney was preoccupied with his personal interests. His evenings were often consumed by gambling and his pursuit of women. If he wasn't on the phone with his bookie, he was chatting up potential dates. His focus was clearly elsewhere, leaving him disengaged from the boys' needs and the responsibilities of his role.

This created a lax and indifferent atmosphere during the evening hours. Typically, the two would retreat to the lounge, where they spent most of their time smoking cigarettes and watching TV. The boys were left to navigate a space where supervision was sporadic and discipline was often inconsistent, a stark contrast to the more structured environment provided earlier in the day.

The few moments of attention Mr. Patrick and Mr. Rodney did give, were often marked by impatience and swift, harsh punishment.

One evening Joe, Ben and I ran down to the second floor to tease the girls. It was a harmless bit of fun, the kind of mischief typical for eight- and nine-year-old boys trying to flirt with their peers. However, one of the girls' counselors had enough of our antics and complained to Mr. Patrick. We were summoned to the lounge "Why can't I watch TV in peace?" Mr. Patrick shouted. His tone left no room for leniency. "Alright, you guys can hang out here with me tonight," he announced. "You're all standing," he added, his voice slurring.

The moment he declared, "You're all standing," a jolt of recognition shot through me. The phrase struck a chord deep within, echoing a past punishment from my mother. Her command of "You're starving" had left a lasting emotional scar. Hearing Mr. Patrick's words triggered a rush of memories and emotions, dredging up the trauma I had associated with that phrase. The similarity in the punitive language made the punishment feel even more daunting and psychologically heavy.

Standing on a chair was a standard form of punishment at the shelter. We were directed to separate corners of the lounge where old, wobbly wooden chairs stood in wait. The punishment was straightforward yet grueling: we were required to stand on these chairs, unable to sit or get down for an hour. For a nine-year-old, maintaining balance on a chair with a seat barely twelve inches wide was a test of endurance. The energy and adrenaline coursing through us made the task nearly impossible.

As the hour dragged on, the monotony of standing on the wobbly chairs began to take its toll. We made eye contact with each other, the shared discomfort and fatigue creating an unspoken bond.

One day bled into the next, as weeks turned into months. Time lost all meaning in that place, where survival was our only goal. We weren't living; we were merely existing, trapped in a limbo where each day felt like a repeat of the last. The institution offered us nothing in the way of stimulation or growth. There were no activities to break up the monotony, no programs to engage our young minds. The hours dragged on, empty and silent, broken only by the harsh voices of the staff and the occasional outburst from a child.

Education, if it could even be called that, was a cruel joke. For a brief moment each day, we were herded into a small room and handed worn-out books. The so-called "reading time" lasted no more than ten minutes—just long enough for them to claim they were doing something for us, but not long enough for us to actually learn. I remember staring at the words on the page, the letters blurring together as I struggled to make sense of them. But how could I focus on reading when all I could think about was how to get through another day?

The rest of the day was a blur of empty hours. We were left to our own devices, wandering the halls or sitting in silence, each of us lost in our own world of confusion and fear. If the weather permitted and the staff deemed it acceptable, we were allowed a brief reprieve in what they called a yard—but to us, it was nothing more than a concrete jungle. The ground was a mess of broken concrete slabs, with jagged pieces of cement scattered across the play area. No more than twenty yards in diameter, the yard bordered by a three foot high wall of cracked bricks. Above it all, a ten-foot-high chain- link fence loomed, a constant reminder of the outside world we were cut off from.

In the morning, the sun would rise over the yard. The warmth of the sunlight attracted flies, which would land on top of the brick wall, basking in comfort. We had little to entertain ourselves with, so the activities boiled down to two things: either climbing on the steel monkey bars, which were set into the broken concrete, or gathering around the brick ledge to swat at the sunbathing flies. While the monkey bars were the only real structure in the yard, they felt like they'd been put there as an afterthought. The steel was always cold. We'd climb, swing, and drop to the ground, trying to pass the time, but the broken concrete below was a constant reminder of the dangers—both seen and unseen—that lurked in every corner of our world.

I never liked the monkey bars. Maybe it was because, like my father, I felt uncomfortable with heights. But one day, I decided I had to conquer the fear.

I climbed to the top, and tried to turn my body to face the other side. At that moment, my foot slipped and I lost my grip. My body twisted in the air, and I felt the hard steel strike my head, arms, and legs as I tumbled down to the concrete base below. I hit the ground with a sickening thud. When I came to, the world was a haze of light and shadow. My head throbbed, my limbs felt heavy, unresponsive. As I lay there, struggling to make sense of what had happened, one of the smaller boys wandered over. Without a second thought, he used me as a step stool to reach the top of the bars, his small feet digging into the small of my back as he climbed.

I spent the rest of the day lying in the yard, wondering just how large the bump on my head would grow. It wasn't until much later that someone finally noticed I was hurt. But by then, the pain had already settled in, a constant reminder of the day I tried—and failed—to conquer my fear.

Chapter 12

A Glimpse of Hope

Several months had passed in that place, months where time seemed to stand still. But one day, out of the blue, I heard news about my parents.

They told me that next weekend, my father was coming to take me on a visit. The word felt foreign to me, like something from another world. A visit. What did that actually mean? Was I going home? Or was this just a temporary escape from the institution's walls?

The night before my first visit, I lay awake in bed, my mind racing. I recalled what had happened the last time my father came to get me. It was Columbus Day, a day that had started with hope and ended in confusion and pain. The memory of that day lingered in my mind like a shadow, casting doubt on what tomorrow would hold.

Would this visit be different? Or would it end up the same way, with me feeling more lost and alone than before?

As I went to breakfast with my group, I moved through the motions like I was on autopilot. I barely touched the food on my plate. The other kids around me were as indifferent as always, each lost in their own world of survival, but for me, this day was different. After breakfast, I left the dining area with the group, feeling like a sheep being herded through the halls and up the stairs. The routine was the same, but my thoughts were elsewhere, focused on what lay ahead.

What did it mean to be taken on a visit? What would my father say? Would he even recognize the boy I had become after all these months? Soon after, one of the staff members approached me, telling me that my father was here, waiting near the front doors. My heart should have leaped at the news, but instead, it stayed steady, weighed down by uncertainty. Rather than run downstairs in blind excitement like a child might, I walked with caution, each step measured.

As I reached the lobby, my eyes quickly scanned the room, and there he was—my father, engaged in conversation with one of the counselors. It was an unusual sight, seeing him there in the flesh after so many months. The distance between us felt both vast and small at the same time. He turned his head in my direction, and our eyes met. In that instant, I felt a connection, a thread tying us together despite everything that had happened. But what struck me most was the look in his eyes of guilt and remorse.

I could see the weight he carried, the burden of whatever had led us to this point. Or maybe he was taken aback by my appearance. Since arriving at Childville I'd lost almost ten pounds. This was not only because of poor food quality, it was also due to the extreme stress and anxiety I've been suffering. I was no longer a healthy young boy from Howard Beach, Queens. I was now a product of institutional life.

As I walked closer to him, my steps slow and measured, I felt like a stray kennel dog meeting their new owner. I offered him a partial smile. It was a smile born out of uncertainty, tinged with caution, as if I wasn't sure whether to embrace this moment or keep my guard up. I wanted to feel the comfort of his presence, the warmth of a father's love, but I also knew that nothing about this visit would be simple. I stood silently as he finished his conversation with the counselor. When he turned to leave, he didn't say anything—just started walking toward the doors with me at his side.

Even though it had been several months since I'd last seen him, it was clear that time hadn't changed some things. As we walked, I half-expected him to reach out, to place a hand on my shoulder, a simple gesture of comfort or connection. But he didn't. My father was never one for physical contact; it wasn't in his nature to offer that kind of reassurance. The space between us felt almost tangible, a reminder of the emotional distance that had always existed.

The cool air hit my face as we descended the slate stairs. My eyes were drawn to the Ford Fairlane parked at the curb. For a moment, a slight smile tugged at the corners of my mouth. That car had once been a symbol of excitement and adventure. I had once seen it as the Batmobile, a vehicle of power and escape. But now, after everything that had happened, it represented something else entirely. It was no longer the car of childhood fantasies but the vehicle of uncertainty, a reminder that the journey ahead was as unpredictable as the one that had brought me to this place.

We drove with no clear destination in mind, until my father finally pulled up in front of a small bodega. "Would you like something from the store?" he asked. "Sure," I replied. Inside, the bodega was a treasure trove of options—candy, soda, cakes—more choices than I had imagined. I was overwhelmed by the selection, each item more appealing than the last. I chose a pack of Yankee Doodles and a bottle of Yoo-hoo.

I set the Yoo-hoo on the floor between my feet and carefully opened the plastic wrapping around the cupcakes. The Yankee Doodles, though simple chocolate cupcakes, were filled with an irresistibly creamy vanilla center. I devoured the first one quickly, savoring every bite before reaching for my bottle of Yoo-hoo. After months of eating basic institutional food, the Yankee Doodles tasted like a world-renowned delicacy.

As I enjoyed my treat, my father glanced down at my sneakers and noted their poor condition. “Let's get you some new sneakers,” he said, pulling away from the curb. We drove to a store named Buster Brown's, its sign featuring a little boy in a funky hat and a bug-eyed dog. The store looked inviting.

The bell above the door jingled softly and we were greeted by a man wearing black-framed glasses and a white jacket, holding a metal measuring device. The sight of the white jacket sent a shiver through me reminding me of the hospital. The man, sensing my discomfort, smiled warmly and greeted us. “Welcome to Buster Brown's, how can I help you today?”- My father explained that we were there for a new pair of sneakers. The man nodded, directed me to sit and measured my foot on the device. “He's a six and a half.”

He returned with a brown box and a lollipop. “Here you go, young man,” he said. The gesture, small and kind, was a welcome distraction. As I removed the wrapper from the lollipop, the man took out a white sneaker from the box. With practiced ease, he lifted my foot and placed the sneaker on it, then threaded the laces into the holes along the sides.

“Okay, take a walk to see how it feels,” he said. I glanced down at the new sneaker, feeling its softness and the unfamiliar weight of fresh soles. The new shoes felt different—better, but also a symbol of the change and uncertainty that lay ahead.

My father and I returned to the car. “Is there anything else you need?” he asked. I hesitated, feeling a wave of embarrassment wash over me. How could I tell him that all my underwear had been stolen from my drawer back at the institution? For the past few days, I had been using my bathing suit as underwear.

I finally said, "Yes, Dad, I need underwear." He nodded, and then carefully locked my new sneakers in the trunk of the car. We walked down the street to a five and dime store where we found some Fruit of the Loom underwear in the boys' department. After about fifteen minutes, we left the store and headed back to the car. But as we approached it, my father noticed that the trunk lid was partially open. He quickly opened it to check inside; the white bag that held my new sneakers was gone. I saw frustration and anger flash across his face. “Let's get out of here,” he muttered in disgust as he opened the car door. I quickly jumped in, and without another word, he accelerated away from the curb. We drove in silence, the earlier excitement of the day replaced by a heavy quiet.

I looked down at my old, worn sneakers, feeling a deep sense of disappointment. Now, all I could do was hope that my battered sneakers would hold out a little longer. Within twenty minutes, we were back in front of Childville. As the car came to a stop, a realization settled over me. I now understood the true meaning of the word “visit.”

After months of not seeing my father, he had come by to spend just a couple hours with me. We drove around the neighborhood, he bought me a snack and some new underwear, and then,—just like that,—he was ready to leave again. His departure was marked by no pat on the back, no hug—only a half-hearted wave as he got back into the car, leaving me standing alone on the slate steps.

I thought to myself that although his visit was fleeting, it was significant that he came to see me rather than the woman who had sent me here. I felt a mix of emotions: confusion, disappointment, and a hollow sense of abandonment.

The visit, brief and seemingly insignificant, had promised a connection I desperately needed but had ultimately failed to deliver. I couldn't help but wonder if this was all I could expect—a few fleeting moments of attention before being left to fend for myself once more.

The day after my father's visit, I told Ben and Joe about it—how it wasn't what I had expected and how it left me feeling more alone than ever. I had hoped that talking about it might ease the disappointment, but instead, I felt a pang of guilt when I noticed the expressions on their faces. They listened quietly, nodding as I recounted the few hours spent with my father. But then I learned something that made my heart sink: neither Joe nor Ben had ever had a visit. Not once. Suddenly, my disappointment seemed small in comparison to what they had been enduring. I had something they longed for—a connection with family, even if it was fleeting and imperfect. It made me appreciate the little I had, even as I grappled with the sadness of it all.

Two days after the visit, after breakfast, we were sent outside again thanks to a streak of nice weather. The yard was packed—kids were on the monkey bars, others lined up along the ledge to swat flies, and a few were tossing a pink Spalding ball back and forth. The ball caught my attention. "Throw it here!" I shouted to a kid holding the ball. He hesitated, eyeing me with uncertainty. I couldn't help but taunt him a little, "What's wrong? You can't reach me!" That did the trick. With a smirk, he hurled the ball—over my head, of course—sending it sailing towards the fence. I sprinted after it, laughing along with the others as I chased the ball down.

For a moment, the gloom of our surroundings lifted, replaced by the simple joy of playing a game in the sun. The ball sat motionless at the foot of the fence's gate.The gate, like the fence, was ten feet high and covered in plastic slats to hinder visibility from the outside. But there was a two-inch gap, just enough to give a sliver of the world beyond. As I bent down to pick up the ball, I heard a voice—a familiar one, soft yet urgent. "Mitchel, Mitchel," it called. I froze, my heart skipping a beat. Slowly, I looked up in the direction of the voice, towards the gap in the fence. There, through the tiny opening, I saw my grandmother's face. Her smile was unmistakable, her eyes sparkling in the sunlight.

I reached out, and our fingers touched through the gate. In that brief, tender moment, all the fear and loneliness I had been carrying seemed to melt away. It was as if her presence, her love, had crossed the barrier to reach me, offering a lifeline when I needed it most. That moment gave me the courage and determination to survive. No matter what lay ahead, I knew I had to keep going—not just for myself, but for the people who loved me and believed in me.

I wondered if I would have made contact with my grandmother that morning if the Spalding ball hadn't ended up against the fence. Did she travel to Williamsburg, every day, peering through the two-inch gap in the institution's fence, hoping that one day I would appear?

Chapter 14

The Silent Guitar

It had been almost seven months since my father had left me on Childville's cold slate doorstep, in October 1966. Seven months of navigating a world that felt both foreign and unkind. I had been subjected to an array of unwarranted punishments, each more arbitrary and cruel than the last. One day, a misplaced comment about the food might lead to hours of meaningless labor. Bullying was a constant, especially from the older kids who ruled the roost with an iron fist.

The month of April took center stage on the calendar, its arrival marked by a tentative promise of a birthday celebration.

Mr. Scott and Ms. Susan gathered everyone for a group announcement: tomorrow will be Mitchel's ninth birthday. Turning nine felt significant, I didn't expect any grand celebrations—this wasn't the place for that.

Mr. Scott pulled me to the side, "What would you like for your birthday?" he asked, his tone unexpectedly gentle. The question caught me off guard. I hadn't prepared for this moment; in fact, I hadn't really expected anyone to ask. Birthdays at Childville were typically just another day, marked only by the passage of time rather than any real celebration. My mind raced as I struggled to think of an answer. As I stood there, silent and uncertain, Mr. Scott broke the silence with a kind suggestion. “Tomorrow, we’ll go into town and check out the stores. Maybe you can find something you’d like.”

His offer was unexpected and somewhat surreal. The idea of going into town, of having the freedom to choose something for myself, was both thrilling and overwhelming. It was a rare opportunity to step outside the confines of Childville and experience a semblance of normalcy. I felt a flicker of hope, tempered by the uncertainty of what the next day might bring.

The following morning, we gathered around the large table for our standard breakfast. The centerpiece was a large steel bowl filled with what was described as scrambled eggs, though in reality, they were powdered eggs, reconstituted with water. They were surprisingly close to the texture and taste of real eggs, though their blandness left much to be desired. The eggs were served using a large, strainer-like spoon, designed to drain the watery excess before the portion was placed on our plates. Alongside the eggs, we were given a couple of slices of toast. The bread was typically dry and plain, but it was a small concession to variety in our otherwise monotonous diet.

Although I didn’t anticipate any special treatment on my birthday, I did feel as if the day itself granted me a brief, silent privilege. Before long, an argument ensued between me and one of the other boys at the table. To my surprise, one of the counselors took his side, delivering a scolding that stung more than I expected. I stormed away from the table, my anger fueling each step as I fled the dining room and sought refuge in the neighboring janitor's closet. There, in the dim, musty space, I sat on the floor beside a bucket of dirty mop water, tears stinging my eyes as I wondered what kind of birthday this was turning out to be.

Despite my absence, the dining room staff emerged from the kitchen carrying a birthday cake with nine candles. From where I huddled on the floor by the bucket, I could hear the excited chatter and laughter as the other kids gathered around the cake, their voices rising in anticipation.

I could almost imagine the scene—hands reaching out, faces lit with joy—while I remained hidden, consumed by my own tears. The sound of candles being extinguished and the clatter of cake being cut felt like a distant celebration, a reminder of the disconnect between my inner turmoil and the world outside.

As the cake was shared among the others, I was left alone in the quiet of the closet, grappling with the painful realization that Childville was not the place to be if you were looking for sympathy.

After everyone left I exited the closet. As I reached the third floor, I saw Mr. Scott and Ms. Susan sitting in the lounge area. They didn't ask where I had been or if I was all right; their relaxed demeanor suggested that my absence was of no concern. It was as if the day continued on its merry way, indifferent to the personal turmoil I was enduring.

Mr. Scott told Ms. Susan he was taking me into town to buy a birthday gift. As we descended the slate steps to the sidewalk, his voice broke the silence with an unexpected question: “Are you excited?” His tone was casual, almost too cheerful, given the cloud of disappointment still hanging over me. I responded with a nod and a smile as we walked towards the corner. A sudden realization struck me—we weren't driving anywhere. We were simply going to stroll through the neighborhood.

“So, what do you think you’d like?” Mr. Scott asked, his voice friendly and curious as we walked along the desolate street towards the stores. He was dressed casually in a baggy tee shirt that draped loosely over his frame. His Ben Hur-style sandals, crunched against the pavement.

We passed the familiar sights of the neighborhood: the corner liquor store, the old laundromat, and the imposing law firm with its stern façade. It quickly became apparent that my options might be limited. Then, up ahead on the next block, I noticed something, a small shop which had three gold balls suspended from a bar in front of its window. The sight of those gleaming orbs made me pause.

“Let's check that out,” I suggested. Mr. Scott followed my gaze, nodding in agreement. As we approached, I noticed the name “Pawnshop” painted in bold red letters across the storefront window. I had learned that a pawnshop was a place where people sold their belongings for quick cash—whether they needed to pay a bill, buy food, or even get a quick fix for an addiction. The concept felt foreign and intriguing to me.

The shop was cluttered but organized, with items neatly arranged on shelves and hanging from display racks.

"This place has everything from the practical to the peculiar," Mr. Scott remarked. "You might just find something unique here." I nodded, my curiosity piqued. Each item seemed to hold a story of its own, and the idea of discovering something special among the assortment was exciting. After a few minutes, a wave of disappointment started to wash over me. Was this really the type of place where I could find a birthday gift? Coffee machines, tools, jewelry—none of these were things I wanted.

Just when I was about to give up, something caught my eye. In the back of the store, hanging prominently on the wall, was a burgundy-colored electric guitar. It looked incredibly cool, like something straight out of a rock star's collection. The only problem was that I didn't know how to play the guitar. I had never held one before, let alone strummed its strings. But there was something about it that captivated me.

As it was handed to me, I felt a thrill of anticipation. I felt its weight and shape. I wasn't sure how to hold it properly, but I mimicked what I had seen on TV. I cradled it gently, positioning it as I had seen Paul McCartney of the Beatles do. Even though I had no clue about how to play it, just holding it felt like stepping into a new world of possibilities. I plucked at the four guitar strings, expecting a rich, resonant chord to fill the room, but was met with silence—no sound, no melody, just an empty void. "Is it broken?" I asked. Mr. Scott gave a reassuring smile and said, "It's an electric guitar. It needs to be plugged into an amplifier to make any sound."

I didn't understand why I was drawn towards this guitar? I never had any desire to play one before nor did I really have any heroes in my life that played the guitar. For a fleeting moment I recalled seeing Sylvester and John playing instruments, John on the guitar and Sylvester on the drums. Was I actually looking up to them?

The idea made me pause. They're just bullies, I told myself. A guitar with no sound—was a clear symbol of my current existence.

Chapter 15

Fruit of the Loom

Only days after my birthday, it was business as usual. Shortly after dinner, the boys were herded up to the third floor to prepare for the evening activities. These activities typically consisted of, either watching Mr. Patrick in a drunken stupor or enduring Mr. Rodney's loud tirades at the television. Returning to our rooms, we undressed in silence, wrapping towels around our waists and slipping into the "shower slippers" we were issued. We shuffled into the community shower, each of us resigned to the process. Our group was only in the shower for a couple of minutes when the plastic curtain was yanked open. Two of the older boys who were following in the footsteps of Sylvester and John had stepped in. My two roommates and I quickly grabbed our towels, eager to escape the shower room. Tony, the stockier of the two, had positioned himself firmly in front of the exit, blocking our path. Meanwhile, Fred, the tall and slim one, approached with a glare.

"Who turned on the showers?" Fred barked, his voice sharp and accusatory. He scanned us with suspicion, as we stood there, in our towels and shower slippers. We exchanged nervous glances, unsure of how to respond. The threat of Fred's ire hung in the air, amplifying the already uncomfortable situation.

Fred placed his hand under the shower spray and frowned. "This is not hot water," he snapped. "You can't shower in warm water; it needs to be hot!" He yanked me roughly by the wrist under the shower head, holding me there with my towel still wrapped around my waist. I tried to resist, but his grip was unrelenting. Without a moment's hesitation, Fred reached for the hot water handle, turning it to the max. Scalding water began to pour down, hitting my skin with a searing intensity. I screamed, desperately trying to pull away to no avail. The steam quickly filled the shower room, swirling around us like a suffocating fog. Fred's chuckle cut through the steam and my cries. "Is it too hot?" he taunted.

As the scalding water continued to pour, he turned off the hot water and cranked up the cold, sending a sharp, icy shock across my already burned skin. The sudden switch from burning heat to numbing cold was excruciating, and my screams grew louder as my body struggled to cope. Fred released his grip on my wrist, and I stumbled backward. My two roommates, who had been watching in stunned silence, quickly moved towards the door. Tony stepped to the side, a cruel smirk as he watched us flee. Once in the safety of our room we huddled together, our breaths coming in ragged gasps. That night, sleep was elusive.

The morning came with a reluctant, gray light seeping through the blinds. Dressing was an ordeal; each motion of pulling on my shirt sent waves of discomfort through my tender skin.

We gathered around the breakfast table, the powdered eggs, an unappetizing but familiar staple, lay in front of us. We ate in silence. The shower incident hung over us, making any attempt at conversation seem inadequate.

After breakfast, Mr. Scott approached me, his expression a mixture of concern and curiosity. He placed his hand delicately on my shoulder. The touch, though gentle, was like a jolt of electricity. I winced involuntarily, trying to mask the discomfort that was evident in my reaction. Mr. Scott's eyes were filled with a searching look, as if he was trying to gauge my true state beneath the facade. His hand remained a moment longer before he withdrew it, his concern genuine but unspoken. "Your father is coming to pick you up for a visit tomorrow," he said with a smile. I nodded, returning the smile with relief and anticipation. As I climbed the stairs back to the third floor, my mind wandered to the last time I had seen him, trying to piece together the months that had passed in the blur of daily life and unspoken challenges.

The following day, as my eyes slowly opened to the morning light, the mysterious underwear thief was finally identified. Since my arrival at Childville, my personal supply of underwear had been the target of a relentless and unwarranted assault. My best efforts—marking my white Fruit of the Looms with my initials— had proved futile. The thief seemed undeterred by my attempts at identification. Underwear, in most places, might be considered a mundane and unremarkable item. But here, in Childville, it took on a significance far beyond its practical use. The stolen underwear had become a symbol of the invasion of privacy that we all felt keenly.

It was one of my roommates. Shock and anger surged through me as I shrieked, "What the hell are you doing?" His head snapped around in surprise, his eyes wide with guilt. "I just needed to borrow a pair, that's all," he replied, his voice defensive as he walked back to his side of the room, clearly attempting to deflect the confrontation. My frustration reached a boiling point. I sprang off the mattress, tackled him, sending us both crashing onto his bed. In a burst of adrenaline and fury, I landed a few clean punches to his face, each hit a release of pent-up frustration. His smug expression quickly shifted to one of pain and shock.

"Take it, take it, I don't need your underwear," he gasped, tossing the items aside in a gesture of surrender. The words, though begrudging, were a small victory. But I wasn't finished. As he turned his back to leave, I acted swiftly. I grabbed him from behind, locking him in a choke hold. His squeals of confusion and panic filled the room as I tightened my grip. With my free hand, I reached towards the back of his waist, pulling at the waistband of his underwear. My initials were clearly visible.

In the next hour, the search through his dresser draw revealed all of my stolen underwear hidden in the back. Each piece retrieved was a small triumph, a reclaiming of my personal space and dignity.

As I gathered the last of the items, a sense of vindication washed over me. The confrontation had been messy, but it was a necessary step in regaining a sense of control. My roommate’s hasty apology and the promise of no further thefts were a meager consolation, but they marked a shift in the balance of power. I had fought back, not just for my belongings but for my own sense of self-respect.

With the stolen items returned, I could finally look forward to my father's visit with a bit more peace of mind.

Chapter 16

The Hat

The following morning, my father appeared right on schedule. Despite his not being the typical family man, my father's consistency provided a form of stability. He wasn't affectionate or involved in the day-to-day minutiae of my life, but he made an effort to be present, a stark difference from my mother's absence. I hadn't seen her in almost a year now, and, surprisingly, it just didn't seem to matter.

As we walked to the car, he broke the silence with a casual question. "So, how was your birthday last week?" The words felt out of place, like a distant echo of concern. I turned to face him, hoping for a moment of connection, only to realize that he wasn't making eye contact. His gaze was fixed straight ahead, I hesitated, hoping that my pause would prompt him to turn his head, to look at me with even the slightest hint of curiosity or engagement. But he continued walking, his expression impassive and his attention directed elsewhere.

I felt a pang of frustration and sadness. The absence of eye contact was a reminder of the emotional chasm that often lay between us, a gap that no amount of small talk could bridge. "Did you get any gifts?" he asked, his tone shifting as if the question was more about filling the silence than genuine curiosity. The abrupt transition from his earlier question caught me off guard. "They bought me a used guitar," I replied, the words feeling flat as they left my mouth. I had received the guitar with a mix of excitement and bewilderment, but it had since remained untouched in the corner of my room.

"A guitar?" he echoed, his voice tinged with surprise. "Why did they get you a guitar? Did you ask for one?" I found myself at a loss for words, struggling to articulate the tangled emotions surrounding the gift. "Honestly, I don't know," I admitted, my voice lacking conviction. "I haven't even touched it since the day I got it. I guess I'm not sure why I asked for it in the first place."

"What can I get you for your birthday?" my father asked. The question, though simple, sparked a sudden shift in my thoughts as I considered what I truly wanted. My mind drifted towards an image that had captivated me recently. It was the guys in the neighborhood, their presence commanding respect and a touch of fear. They walked the streets with a certain gang-like attitude. The common bond among them was a distinctive accessory: a beaver skin cap.

Some caps were worn in their natural, rugged state, while others were meticulously treated with Vaseline.

The treatment created a shiny, circular pattern on the surface, reflecting the light in subtle ways. I realized how much I wanted one. It wasn't just about the hat but the sense of identity and belonging it represented, a symbol of a different kind of confidence and style. "I'd like one of those beaver skin caps," I said.

My father glanced at me, "A beaver skin cap?" he repeated. With a shrug, he started to drive. It seemed he had a destination in mind, and as we ventured further, the streets began to change. The once familiar surroundings of Childville gave way to more densely populated areas, and I could feel a shift in the environment.

The contrast was striking. The streets grew busier, alive with activity and energy. The sidewalks were lined with bustling shops, street vendors, and a diverse array of people going about their daily routines. The vibrant atmosphere was a far cry from the subdued and constrained life at Childville. My father maneuvered into a parking spot, and I saw a large storefront across the street displaying an impressive array of hats. The sign in front read "Knox Hats."

Prominent in the window; were several beaver skin hats—just like the ones I had seen on the guys from the neighborhood. "Looks like you're in luck," my father said with amusement.

Although the hats were displayed in their natural condition, with short, dry, wavy hair, I knew that a small touch of Vaseline would bring it to life. The thought of transforming the hat myself, applying the Vaseline and combing it in, added an extra layer of excitement to the process. I selected a navy blue cap. The hat was placed into a special box, its polished surface hinting at the potential it held.

As we made our way back to the car, I glanced at the box in my hands, thrilled. The cap seemed almost alive, and I was eager to transform it into something uniquely my own.

My father, who had been watching my enthusiasm from the sidelines, finally allowed a genuine smile to break through his usual reserve. It was clear that he was pleased. There was a warmth in his expression that I hadn't seen often—a reflection of his satisfaction in making his son happy.

As we drove, the energy of the city began to fade, giving way to darker, more subdued surroundings. My father pulled up in front of the familiar bodega we had visited. Before exiting the car, I made sure to take the hatbox with me, a precautionary move after the unfortunate mishap with my new sneakers on our last visit. I didn't want to risk anything happening to my prized new hat.

As I stepped out, my father noticed the box in my hands. He smiled and nodded approvingly, an acknowledgment of how much the hat meant to me. With a sense of purpose, I entered the bodega. With my new hat, Yankee Doodles, and Yoo-hoo in hand, I felt ready to return to Childville with a newfound sense of assurance and excitement.

Shortly after being dropped off by my father, I started showing off my new hat. I put it on and paraded around the institution, getting compliments from everyone who saw it. It still wasn't perfect, though: I needed to apply the vaseline. One of the Spanish kids that roomed next to me got my attention saying "My friend just got one of those hats, he had me put the vaseline on. If you want I can do yours." I turned to him; "Really?

You put the vaseline on it?" The kid shook his head, a smile tugging at the corners of his mouth. "Yep, I did it, do you want me to do yours?" he asked, his eyes twinkling with a mix of confidence and sincerity.

I hesitated for a moment. The idea of handing over my prized hat to someone else made me uneasy, but the thought of having it done perfectly, just as I envisioned, was tempting. I agreed. My plan was to hover and watch his every move. He carefully spread the vaseline, smoothing it over the hat's surface with a practiced hand.

Within thirty minutes, the hat was transformed. It looked amazing—sleek, glossy, impeccable. I admired the way it caught the light, reflecting a perfect sheen that made it stand out even more. I turned to my new friend; "Thanks a lot," I said. "It looks great!" He gave a modest shrug, clearly pleased. "No problem," he said, displaying a look of accomplishment. I set off down the halls, feeling a renewed sense of confidence. I caught the eyes of others. Their reactions were as enthusiastic as before, but now there was an extra layer of admiration.

After securing permission to step out of the institution for a few minutes, I exited through the large wooden doors and descended the slate steps. With a new sense of strength and pride, I began to strut down the desolate sidewalk. The feeling of the hat perched confidently on my head infused me with a boldness I hadn't fully experienced before. Each step felt deliberate and strong, as if I were marking my territory in this unfamiliar world.

I turned a corner onto a block that was empty, the only sounds being the swaying of empty trash cans lying on their side. The street seemed to stretch on indefinitely, amplifying the sense of solitude and independence that I felt.

As I continued walking, a movement caught my attention from across the street. I glanced over and saw a teenager walking on the sidewalk parallel to me. Though there was no immediate threat, I kept a wary eye on him as I proceeded, my senses heightened.

I kept checking to see if he was still there, but to my surprise, he disappeared from view. I stopped for a moment, scanning the area to see where he might have gone. The street was empty, and I couldn't spot him anywhere. Puzzled and still on edge, I continued cautiously toward the corner.

Suddenly, I felt a sharp rush of wind as my hat was lifted off my head. I turned around to see the same teenager, who had somehow crossed the street and hidden behind a parked car. With the stealth of a predator, he had crept up behind me and snatched the hat from my head. In shock, I watched as he dashed down the street, the hat clutched triumphantly in his hand. I took off after him, but he was much quicker. Soon he was out of sight, leaving me standing in the middle of the street, breathless and defeated.

I returned to the shelter, embarrassed and angry. A symbol of my pride and confidence—had been stolen. I could almost feel the hat slipping through my fingers again, the sense of control and satisfaction I had briefly experienced now replaced by helplessness.

The other residents went about their routines, some glancing my way with curiosity as I walked in, my expression likely revealing my turmoil.

I found a quiet spot and tried to steady myself. The day's events replayed in my mind, each moment of triumph now intertwined with the sting of defeat. It was a harsh reminder of how fleeting moments of pride can be and how quickly they can be overshadowed by setbacks.

Chapter 17

The Picture

Spring turned into summer. The monotony of life at the shelter was stifling; despite the changing seasons, everything remained the same. The yard offered only the monkey bars for entertainment, the common area had a television, and beyond that, your friends were your only solace.

One afternoon, I glanced over at the electric guitar resting in the corner. It had been several months since Mr. Scott took me to the pawn shop to buy it and since then, I hadn't touched it.

What should I do with it? Heading toward the common area, I passed Sylvester and John's room. I glanced in. Everything was the same—the painting on the wall, the faded carpet and the wooden lamps on the nightstands. Their instruments were lined neatly along the wall.

I continued to the common area and took a seat in front of the TV, though I wasn't really paying attention to it. My mind kept drifting back to my guitar. What was I going to do with it? After daydreaming in front of the TV for a while, I made up my mind. First, though, I had to wait for Sylvester and John to return. Whatever came next, it would start with them.

I heard laughter from the stairs; it was Sylvester and John. I watched them disappear to their room, my mind racing. The time had come to follow through on my decision. I waited a few minutes, giving them time to settle in, then got up and walked down the hallway. Their door was slightly ajar, just enough for me to stand in the doorway and stare. I cleared my throat, and they both looked up at me, their conversation falling silent. Before they could say anything, I spoke up. "I have a deal for you." Their stern expressions softened instantly. They exchanged amused glances before bursting into laughter, clearly finding my timing and tone entertaining.

"Oh yeah?" Sylvester said, "What kind of deal are we talking about?" John leaned back, crossing his arms. "Let's hear it then. What's your deal?" Their easy going demeanor made me feel more at ease. I took a deep breath, ready to pitch whatever this deal was, it had to be worth their attention.

"I have an expensive electric bass guitar I want to trade," I said, keeping my tone serious. John's eyebrows went up. "Where is it?" he asked, arms still folded.

"It's in my room. I'll get it," I replied, turning and walking down the hall towards my door. I picked it up from the floor, brushing off the dust with my hands as I made my way back. I could hear them talking quietly, their voices tinged with interest. The knowledge that they were intrigued gave me a boost of confidence.

When I reached their door, I walked in without hesitation, despite knowing that entering their room under any circumstances resulted in a beating. I brought the guitar to John, who examined it closely. "Wow, it's a classic bass," he said to Sylvester, both of them now inspecting it with genuine interest.

John walked over to his amplifier and plugged it in, starting with a few quick tests of the strings. As he played, his head bobbed with the rhythm, and soon he was tapping his toe and grinning. "Okay, what do you want?" he asked, still fiddling with the guitar.

At that moment, I knew I had him. I squared my shoulders and said, "All I want is the picture on your wall, the rug, and one lamp." John glanced over at Sylvester for confirmation, as the picture and rug were theirs collectively. After a brief exchange, John turned back to me and said, "Deal!" He removed the picture and its hook from the wall and carried it into my room along with one of the lamps and the faded area rug. "Oh, just one last thing," I added, trying to sound as firm as possible. "You will no longer target me or my two friends, Joe and Ben, anymore." John looked at me, his expression serious, and then nodded in agreement. "You've got it."

Leaving their room, I felt triumphant. The new arrangement was set, and for once, things felt more balanced. I knew full well that the guitar was worth far more than their shabby picture, lamp, and rug. But to me, it wasn't about the money. It was about status. Those items had been part of Sylvester and John's space for years, a small part of their territory and influence. Now, they were mine.

I sat on my bed and thought about the arrangement, savoring the victory. First, I rolled out the faded area rug, smoothing it between my bed and the wall. There was no way I was going to share this item of authority with my roommate—it was mine now, a symbol of the deal I had made. Next, I hung the picture on the wall, carefully positioning it just above the rug. The colors looked a bit dull, but that didn't matter.

Last, I placed the wooden lamp on my nightstand, I sat back and admired my new environment.

The room felt different—no longer just a space I existed in, but one where I held a little more control. The rug, the picture, the lamp… all small things, but together, they shifted something inside me.

As I sat there, a couple of kids passed by my door, their footsteps slowing as they peeked in. I saw the flicker of surprise in their eyes as they noticed the picture on my wall—the same picture that had hung in Sylvester and John's room for years. I met their looks with one of quiet confidence, holding their gaze for a moment. In that exchange, I could feel it—an acknowledgment of the shift. Where they had once seen just another kid in the hall, now they saw someone who had made a bold move.

It soon became clear that Sylvester and John's time at Childville was nearing its end. I saw them less frequently, only catching glimpses of them as we passed in the hall, kitchen, or common area.

Our interactions had shifted. There were no more words, no need for conversation—just a nod and a smile. That simple gesture became our form of communication, a silent acknowledgment of the bond we'd forged through that trade.

Before the first snowfall in the winter of 1967, they were both gone. No fanfare marked their departure. There was no party, no grand celebration to acknowledge the years they had spent at Childville—just another empty room.

I stepped inside the vacant room and stared, I still felt a twinge of caution. Even though they were gone, their room held onto that aura of dominance, as if their presence had left an imprint on the space. The bare walls, the empty floor—everything seemed hollow, yet the weight of their time there still lingered.

I stood for a moment, absorbing it, before retreating to my own room. When I entered and saw the picture hanging on my wall, I smiled. That picture, once a symbol of their control, was now mine, and with it came a story I would never forget.

Chapter 18

Childville Chess

As winter approached, I felt a change in the dynamic. I was no longer the wide-eyed newbie; my friends and I had found our place. We weren't leaders, nor were we feared by anyone, but we were no longer at the bottom of the pecking order. We had settled somewhere in the middle, a comfortable position where we could navigate without too much attention. With this new standing came certain opportunities. One was becoming a "kitchen helper." It wasn't glamorous—essentially serving during mealtimes and cleaning off the tables afterward—but the small payment made it worthwhile. And it came with unexpected perks. Up until then, I'd assumed the endless supply of powdered eggs and dry toast was the only breakfast option at Childville. But working in the kitchen gave me access to the giant refrigerator, where hidden treasures were stashed away. Real food—bacon, sausage, fresh fruit—was right there, waiting to be discovered. I quickly realized that being a kitchen helper wasn't just a job; it was an opportunity to get more than the usual bland meals.

Mr. Young, the cook, was a middle-aged Black man with a warm heart and a no-nonsense attitude. As long as you were there to work and not to fool around, he welcomed you. After everyone had cleared out of the dining room and the tables were wiped down, he'd ask us what we wanted for breakfast.

One morning, I noticed real eggs sitting by the stove—an unexpected luxury. But what really caught my eye was something strange-looking: a brown, foot-long tube, about two inches in diameter. I kept staring at it, trying to figure out what it was. Noticing my curiosity, Mr. Young asked, "Would you like to try a piece of salami?" He sliced a piece off the end and tossed it onto the grill. I nodded, fascinated, watching as the salami sizzled and browned on the hot surface. The smell was rich and savory, completely different from the dry toast and powdered eggs I was used to.

Mr. Young slid the salami onto a small plate for me. I picked it up and bit off a small piece. It was like nothing I'd ever eaten before—rich, salty, and slightly crisp around the edges. I was sold and immediately asked for more. Mr. Young chuckled and tossed another slice on the grill.

As the winter cold settled in, it seemed to wrap itself around our lives like an uninvited guest. The yard lay dormant under a blanket of snow. Board games, once occasional diversions, now took center stage in our daily lives.

Checkers and chess were no longer just games; they became our battlegrounds of strategy and wit. They soon evolved into arenas of dominance and control.

While everyone at the shelter experienced moments of being outmaneuvered or outplayed, such instances were seen as blemishes on one's character. To be a victim, even in the realm of a board game, was to risk being perceived as weak. Thus, the games took on a new significance: they became a means of staking your claim, of asserting your place in the hierarchy of Childville.

One of the boys, face flushed with anger, accused his opponent of cheating. The accused, caught off guard, responded with an immediate denial. His reaction, a poorly veiled attempt to deflect the blame. The room erupted into chaos as the other players—eager for a distraction from their own struggles for dominance—rallied behind the accuser.

What started as a heated dispute quickly escalated. Normally, verbal banter was not a precursor to physical attacks in Childville. Here, being ready to defend yourself at all times was more than just a precaution; it was a necessity. The shelter's atmosphere demanded constant vigilance, where any hint of weakness or hesitation could trigger an immediate and aggressive response.

In this charged environment, shouting and accusations quickly gave way to more direct confrontations. Hands which previously manipulated chess pieces now clenched into fists, and words turned into shoves.

In the blink of an eye, the accuser lunged, seizing his cheating opponent by the waist. With a fierce shove, he drove him against the radiator mounted on the wall. The metal hissed as steam erupted from its battered surface. The cheater was now pinned down, the small of his back making contact with the steel slats of the radiator. The radiator panged as it spit steam into the hostile air that surrounded the attack. Two of the counselors burst into the room, their footsteps pounding against the wooden floor. The counselors moved swiftly to separate the attacker from his target.

With a forceful grip, they pried the attacker's hands away from the cheater, who was slumped against the radiator, his back marked with angry red burns. As the attacker was pulled away, the cheater was quickly escorted to the nurse's office, his every step a testament to the pain he endured.

Meanwhile, the attacker was not spared from the consequences of his actions. He was led to the TV room, where he was placed on one of the wobbly chairs, where he spent the next hour shifting and balancing uncomfortably. A physical reminder of the price of his aggression.

The winter holidays and festivities at Childville were uneventful, marked by a stark and sterile environment that did little to lift the spirits of those within its walls. The usual cheer of the season was muted by the shelter's cold atmosphere. Decorations were sparse, and any semblance of celebration was overshadowed by the routine of daily life.

The dreariness of winter slowly gave way to the arrival of spring in 1968 bringing with it the faint promise of renewal and life. Yet, even as the world outside began to awaken, a sense of melancholy lingered within me. Though I wasn't heartbroken, it had been a while since the last time I'd seen my father. The distance between us felt both physical and emotional. His absence was a constant presence in my life, a void that was highlighted by the changing seasons.

Chapter 19

The Cottages

My friends and I looked forward to spending springtime in the yard. Not that there were any flowers blooming or grass growing; the yard remained as stark and barren as ever. But the arrival of spring meant one simple pleasure: the warmth of the sun on the cold, hard cement.

That spring, I learned that Childville had hired a new teacher. The previous teacher had been more of a "babysitter" than an educator whose role seemed to consist solely of keeping an eye on us and ensuring we didn't get into too much trouble. Attempts at structured learning were minimal, leaving much of our time unengaged and unproductive.

In April 1968, as I approached my tenth birthday, the realization hit me: my education had been virtually non-existent. Up until this point, my experience with formal schooling ended at age seven. Since then, my learning has been sporadic at best, with no consistent instruction or structured curriculum. The arrival of the new teacher brought a glimmer of hope. The prospect of actual education, rather than mere supervision, was both exciting and daunting. I had longed for a sense of normalcy and the chance to learn beyond the confines of the shelter's walls.

The new teacher focused on reading. Despite being ten years old, I struggled with reading at a seven-year-old's level. It showed how far behind I was. This struggle was not unique to me; it was the case for most ten-year-olds in the shelter. The lack of consistent education and meaningful instruction had left us all at a significant disadvantage. The new teacher's efforts were met with varying degrees of success. For many of us, the task felt overwhelming. But thanks to the new teacher's dedication, within a couple of months, I made progress and started to approach my required reading level.

In addition to the arrival of the new teacher, we were informed that the summer would bring a special "getaway" designed for all ages at the shelter. First, the eight-and nine-year-olds would go on their trip, then, the ten- and eleven-year-olds, and so on. This announcement quickly became the talk of the shelter. The idea of a getaway was nothing short of exhilarating.

After a few weeks of patient waiting, the day of our trip arrived. The night before we left, Mr. Scott gathered us for a briefing about our destination and what we could expect. His tone was upbeat and reassuring. He began by telling us that the journey would be over an hour long, then revealed the details of our destination: a couple of cottages nestled in the middle of the woods, alongside a gentle stream. We would be staying there for two weeks.

For me, this was an entirely new experience. The only place I had previously visited was the World's Fair, certainly not as natural as the cottages. The prospect of staying in the woods, surrounded by nature, felt like a gift. I imagined the rustic charm of the cottages, the rustle of leaves, and the soothing sound of the stream.

The next day, we arrived at our destination. The bus crept along a narrow dirt road, maneuvering around the low-hanging branches of trees. The road was rugged, covered in a mix of stones and uneven patches, adding to the sense of adventure. As the bus rounded a bend, the cottages came into view, like a scene from a dream. They were nestled in the woods, serene and inviting. The sight was enough to make us all leap from our seats, eager to be the first out the door. When the bus finally came to a stop, we tumbled out onto the grass, our feet finally touching the ground after the long ride. We ran towards the open field that lay before us.

Our laughter and cheers filled the air as we ran in circles, reveling in the freedom and the new surroundings. The open field stretched out around us, a vast expanse of grass and earth that seemed to go on forever. We sprinted and twirled, our smiles wide and energy boundless. The joy of running freely in such a beautiful setting was exhilarating.

Eventually, we collapsed onto the grass, our breaths coming in heavy but satisfied gasps. Running, laughing, and enjoying the new environment—this was a pure, unfiltered happiness that we hadn't experienced in a long time.

As the driver and the counselors carried our bags to the cottages, I wandered over to the stream with a couple of other boys. It was a tranquil sight: clear, cool water flowing gracefully over shiny, smooth rocks. The sound of the water babbling over the stones was soothing. The sun dappled through the trees, casting playful shadows on the water's surface.

One of the boys knelt beside the stream, dipping his hand into the refreshing water. As he did, a small frog suddenly leaped from the edge of the stream and landed on a rock nearby. We all stopped and stared in awe at the frog, which seemed just as curious about us. It sat poised on the rock, its small, beady eyes observing us with a kind of deliberate calm, unperturbed. We watched in silent fascination, marveling at the creature's stillness and the natural beauty surrounding us. The frog's sudden appearance felt like a gift.

After a while, I walked back to the field with a boy named Tom. We noticed two bows and a few arrows leaning up against a tree. Although I had never tried shooting an arrow before, it looked simple enough. The arrows had round metal tips on the ends, not the sharp, dangerous kind. We only had three arrows between us, so I stayed at one end of the field while Tom ran about thirty yards away, facing me. We took turns shooting the arrows toward each other. I shot the three arrows first, then Tom would shoot them back. It felt like a harmless game—back and forth, over and over—until it got boring.

To make it more exciting, we started shooting them into the air, taking turns watching them arc high above us before retrieving them. After a while, I took aim at the sky and shot the arrow up. My eyes followed its path as it appeared to be traveling down towards Tom.

Tom just stood there, he never moved, watching the arrow come down as if mesmerized. My heart skipped a beat when I realized it wasn't going to miss him. Before I could yell out, the arrow struck him on the side of his head. His scream cut through the stillness of the field. He grabbed the side of his head and started crying. Panicked, I ran over to him, my stomach twisting into knots. To my relief, the arrow hadn't pierced his skin, but he cried loudly enough to draw the attention of the counselors.

They rushed over, their faces hard with concern. One of them knelt down, asking him what had happened. Without missing a beat, he pointed his finger at me and said, "He shot me with the arrow." I tried to explain. It was an accident. I didn't mean for the arrow to hit him, and he wasn't even hurt. But it didn't matter.

The counselors didn't ask any more questions. One of them gave me a look that said it all—disappointment, anger, maybe even a little disgust. I watched as he walked over to the cabin, grabbed my bag, and slung it over his shoulder. Without a word, he marched to the bus, my bag bouncing against his side. I trailed behind him, heart pounding, knowing what was coming next. The bus door opened with a hiss, and he tossed my bag inside before motioning for me to follow. I didn't even get a chance to say goodbye to the other kids. The game had gone wrong, and now I was being punished. As I sat down on the cold bus seat, staring out the window at the field, a sense of disbelief settled over me. It had all happened so fast. Just minutes ago, we were playing, and now I was alone on the bus, waiting for whatever punishment was coming next. It was one more reminder of how quickly things could turn in a place like this—how one small mistake could lead to bigger consequences than I ever expected.

A few minutes later, the driver and one of the counselors boarded the bus. I could hear their quiet conversation, but the words didn't register. All I could focus on was the heaviness in my chest, the growing realization that I was being sent back to Childville, though I wasn't sure what awaited me. We began the slow ride down the dirt road toward the highway. I didn't bother looking back.

I lay down across the seat as my body gave in to exhaustion. An hour later, I woke up to the familiar streets of Williamsburg, a sharp contrast to the woods and stream I had left behind. The buildings felt as cramped and worn down as I remembered. My stomach tightened as we neared building number 130, Childville looming ahead like a shadow. The bus slowed to a stop, I sat there for a second. No one was waiting to greet me—just the building, cold and indifferent, like it didn't care if I came or went.

The counselor handed me my bag without a word. The driver didn't make eye contact as I stepped off the bus, I climbed the slate stairs, pushed open the wooden door, and began my slow trek to the third floor.

The building seemed even quieter than usual. I noticed Mr. Patrick, asleep on the worn couch in the lounge. His snores filled the stillness of the room, he didn't stir as I walked by. Three of the bedrooms, just like mine, were empty. They were all still at the cottage—the place I had just come from. None of the beds were made—no sheets, no blankets—just the exposed plastic. We weren't supposed to be here. We were meant to be away for two weeks, enjoying the cottage and the break from this place. But here I was, alone in an empty room.

As I changed into my pajamas, my tears started to fall. I didn't bother wiping them away. There was no one here to see me cry, and even if there had been, I wasn't sure I would've cared. As I settled down, I noticed the faint yellow stain in the center of the bed—a reminder of the countless kids who'd slept on it before me, all with their own struggles, their own fears. I shifted uncomfortably, trying to angle my body around the stain, but it didn't matter. No position felt right. The bed was as uncomfortable as my thoughts, hard and unforgiving.

I woke up the next morning to an unusual silence. The absence of the usual early morning squabbles, which I often found grating, felt oddly unsettling. I lay there in bed, straining to catch any sound—anything that would reassure me that the world was still turning as it should.

Making my way down the hall, I spotted Mr. Scott in one of the lounge chairs. A sinking feeling told me that this encounter might not end well for me. Upon seeing me, Mr. Scott rose from his chair and positioned himself directly in front of me. "I heard what happened yesterday," he said, his voice tinged with a hint of sorrow. "First, I must apologize," he continued, slightly dipping his head. "I received a phone call this morning from the counselor who put you on the bus. Last night, before Tom went to bed, he spoke with the same counselor about the incident. Tom said it was all his fault—it was just a harmless game. He mentioned that you never intended to hurt him; he wanted to scc how closc hc could gct to the falling arrow."

"Unfortunately, the bus isn't scheduled to return to the camp area for two weeks for pick-up," Mr. Scott added, his expression reflecting genuine regret. "Otherwise, I would have sent you back right away. I'm really sorry for the situation you've been put in." I felt a wave of relief wash over me, as I felt somewhat vindicated. Yet, as the initial satisfaction faded, I couldn't shake the sense of loss. Despite the resolution, the damage lingered.

Chapter 20

The Bodega

During the following two weeks, I grappled with isolation. While my friends were enjoying themselves at the cottages, I spent hours alone in the yard, aimlessly kicking around broken chunks of concrete. I found myself drawn to the gap in the fence, wondering if my grandmother might be waiting for me on the other side. Time had taken its toll, and I couldn't help but question what the future held.

My tenth birthday had come and gone with little fanfare: there were no parties, no electric guitars—just a small cake with a single candle served after my powdered egg breakfast. The contrast between the celebrations I had imagined and the reality of my solitude was disheartening. Although I was now ten, my physique was largely unchanged. I was slightly taller, but I weighed the same, if not less, than the previous year. As I grappled with the onset of depression, it seemed that my physical well-being was also beginning to deteriorate. The external signs of my aging were minimal, but internally, I felt a growing disconnect, both emotionally and physically, marking a troubling shift in my overall health.

I couldn't recall the last time I had seen my father. While our visits had been brief and devoid of emotional connection, they still fulfilled a lingering need for family. In contrast, my mother had become a distant memory. The following morning, as the buses arrived, I watched from the window while they unloaded. Laughter and smiles filled the air, a clear sign that the two-week adventure had provided a therapeutic lift to everyone's spirits. This enhanced the distance I felt from their renewed vitality.

Joe and Ben had heard about what happened at the cottages, how Tom's lies had led to my being sent back. I felt a twinge of relief when I learned that they had roughed him up a little in response. As they recounted their trip—catching frogs at the stream, playing frisbee, spending a night sleeping in the woods—I could sense their excitement and joy. I understood their enthusiasm, much like how I had felt when I talked about my brief visits with my father. Their stories provided a glimpse into a world I had missed, just as my own experiences had been a bittersweet escape for me.

Over the next few weeks, I began to notice a lot of new faces around Childville. As the older kids were being shipped out, younger ones were brought in. New faces wandered the yard, their expressions uncertain, concerned, and fearful. I watched with unease as some of the older kids surveyed the new arrivals with a predatory gaze. The cycle of intimidation and vulnerability continued.

I was overwhelmed by a profound sense of abandonment. It felt as though a whole year had passed with no sign of my father, leaving me to grapple with a deepening worry about my future. The thought that I might remain at the shelter until I too was removed due to age; weighed heavily on me. In addition, my health was becoming increasingly concerning. My body remained undernourished, and my weight was well below average, making me resemble a modern-day holocaust survivor. Visiting the shelter's doctor was not a viable option; my condition would likely be attributed to poor care, something the institution was reluctant to address. This neglect compounded my sense of dread and helplessness, leaving me to grapple with both my physical and emotional struggles in isolation.

Just as the fall season was approaching, I was advised that my father was coming for a visit the next day. I couldn't decide what I desired most, seeing my father or getting a pack of Yankee Doodles with a Yoo-hoo. At this point nothing seemed to matter anymore. I begged for the chance to be a kitchen helper driven by a craving for real food. The following morning, Mr. Young prepared salami and eggs for me, which I devoured if it were my last meal. I consumed each bite with a fervent appreciation that reflected my yearning for something substantial and satisfying amidst the routine of shelter life.

After finishing my dining room chores I walked towards the stairs. Just as I reached for the banister the front door creaked open and my father walked in. Our eyes locked as we shared a moment of what appeared to be compassion. My father looked slightly concerned if not confused; as I walked towards him his hand reached out and touched my shoulder. This was a monumental gesture–he had made physical contact with me! I don't know why he released a sudden wave of emotion at that moment. I can only assume that he was caught off guard by my frail appearance.

I saw a hint of red, covering the whites of his eyes. It was a sign of something deep, a weariness that spoke volumes. I wondered how long he had been carrying the burdens that etched lines of concern across his face. In that moment, the familiar walls between us fclt likc thcy might finally crack. I continued to watch as the index finger of his right hand swept a partial tear from his eye. The gesture struck me, revealing a vulnerability I had seldom seen. We walked outside to the Ford. My father paused at the passenger door, and allowed me to enter first. I slid into the seat, the familiar scent of old leather wrapping around me like a comforting blanket, a small reminder of home in this tumultuous moment.

As he settled into the driver's seat, I couldn't shake the feeling that something profound was unfolding between us. I assumed we were headed for the bodega, our unspoken routine providing a thin layer of comfort. Once there, I got my familiar pack of Yankee Doodles and a Yoo-hoo. Back in the car, my father pivoted in his seat, now almost facing me.

"There are going to be some changes soon," he stated, his voice steady as he attempted to make eye contact. I slowly sipped the Yoo-hoo, the sweet, chocolate flavor momentarily distracting me. He continued to outline his plans, talking about new opportunities and ideas for improvement, but his words faded into a blur. I was not ready to listen or accept what felt like false hope for my future. Instead, I focused on the sign which hung above the store outside, wondering what the word 'Bodega' meant. My thoughts were consumed by uncertainty. Change felt overwhelming, and I wasn't sure I could trust his intentions. The last time he had promised improvement, it had led to disappointment.

Our visit seemed to end shortly after it started. We drove around as my father purged what was bothering him, his words spilling out like a breaking dam. I tried to appear interested, nodding at the appropriate moments, but deep down, I had already shut down. The truth loomed heavy in my mind: the end result was going to be the same. Shortly after our drive, I would be returned to the slate steps of Childville, just like a stray dog being brought back to the kennel. Resignation and anxiety gnawed at my insides.

I spent the remainder of that day trying to recall what my father had said, desperately reaching for a glimmer of hope for my future. But my mind was lost in a sea of confusion, his words jumbled and tangled like a broken puzzle. I replayed our conversation over and over, hoping to find something that would anchor me, something that could break through the fog of doubt.

As the days and weeks drifted by, I lost all hope in my father's plan. Each promise of change felt more distant than the last, slipping away like leaves falling from the trees. The seasons began to change again, and the cold air shot through the yard, whistling as it blew between the vinyl slats in the fence. At this point, I felt as if I was giving up. There was clearly not going to be a rainbow waiting for me at the end of the storm. My health, both physical and emotional, was suffering, weighed down by the relentless strain of my surroundings. I was exhausted, not just from the bullying and the uncertainty of life in

Childville, but from the constant effort to muster hope. The laughter that used to come so easily with my friends now felt forced, a thin veneer over the growing despair.

The hope I once held that my father would rescue me from this nightmare was fading fast.

Chapter 21

The Bow Wow

The spring of 1970 was in full bloom when Mr. Scott and Ms. Susan told me to follow them into a small private room. I stepped inside and took a seat. They exchanged a glance that seemed to carry weight, as if they were sharing a moment of understanding. I could sense the tension in the air, and wondered what this meeting was really about.

"Mitchel, you're going home!" Mr. Scott said, a big smile spreading across his face. Confusion washed over me. "Do you mean going on a visit?" I asked, staring into their eyes, searching for clarity. "No, Mitchel. You're leaving Childville!" they confirmed, as they approached my chair and hugged me tightly. In that moment, a rush of emotions surged within me, overwhelming my senses. I couldn't contain it any longer; tears streamed down my face as I slid off the chair and curled up into a ball on the floor. The weight of my struggles, the loneliness, and the longing for a place to call home all poured out in a cascade of relief and disbelief. They knelt beside me, their presence a comforting anchor in the storm of my emotions. I felt their hands on my back, gentle and reassuring, but the reality of the news was still too much to process. I was finally going home—after three and a half years of unwarranted abuse, I was finally being given a chance to leave this place behind.

I was given about a week to transition. The news was unexpected. First I spoke with Joe and Ben. I wanted to share my excitement, but I was also keenly aware of their feelings. I made sure they understood that they would always be my friends, regardless of where I was. I presented them with my prized possessions, the items I had received from Sylvester and John in exchange for my guitar. It felt like a way to reclaim a piece of myself, turn something that had once caused pain into a source of connection. Together, we carefully arranged the items–the rug, the picture, and the lamp stood as a beacon of our friendship. Although the shadows of Sylvester and John lingered in my mind, I felt a sense of closure as we admired the setup.

As I walked through Childville for the last time, I revisited some of the locations that would haunt me forever. I wandered into the yard and drifted toward the fence. My eyes fixated on the two-inch gap in the gate, a memory embedded in my mind—still searching for Rebecca. When she appeared, it was a spark of hope in the darkness. But as quickly as she had come, I watched her leave, and the pain of that goodbye lingered.

"Mitchel!" Mr. Scott called out, pulling my gaze from the gap in the fence. I turned to see him standing there, a look of encouragement on his face, and for a moment, the weight of my past faded away.

As I stepped toward him, I felt the tension of the moment shift, the air filled with a sense of hope that this eleven and a half year old hadn't felt in a long time. The world beyond Childville was opening up. Mr. Scott escorted me to the front door where my father waited, already holding my suitcase—originally a symbol of despair and abandonment, now a tangible representation of my new beginning.

My father shook hands with Mr. Scott. Turning to me, my face displayed a partial smile, one that I understood as welcoming. I sensed that perhaps, just perhaps, this could be the start of something different.

Mr. Scott patted me on the back, radiating warmth, as if he believed I had already accomplished a significant journey in life. His gesture filled me with a sense of validation that I hadn't realized I needed. As I waved goodbye to him, I noticed he was wearing the same sandals he had on the day I arrived—Columbus Day in 1966. That detail reminded me of how far I had come since then. With a final wave, I turned to my father, ready to embrace whatever lay ahead, carrying the lessons from Childville with me into this new chapter.

He pushed open the large wooden entrance door, which creaked, with the same sound it had made over three years ago when we first arrived. The familiar noise stirred a wave of nostalgia within me reminding me of the countless moments that had unfolded within those walls.

I sat comfortably in the passenger seat as my father started up the car. Unlike over three years ago, when I was full of eagerness and courage as Robin, today I felt a tinge of caution and uncertainty. I believe it was at this moment that the Batmobile was gone forever.

I thought of the times we had raced through Gotham City in that iconic vehicle, the streets alive with possibility. Now, everything felt different. The shadows seemed longer, the stakes higher. Although this was a very big day, the silence felt heavy. I shifted my gaze between my father and the passing scenery, my thoughts swirling. Were we really headed home to Howard Beach, or was he about to take me somewhere I didn't want to go?

"Everything okay?" he finally broke the silence.

I nodded, but my heart raced. I could read the tension in his posture, the way his knuckles gripped the steering wheel. I wanted to ask where we were really going, but the words stuck in my throat. After a while, the surroundings began to mirror my thoughts of Howard Beach. As we turned onto Crossbay Blvd, a sense of familiarity washed over me. I felt my heartbeat quicken with each landmark we passed, memories flooding back.

Then, I spotted it—the Bow Wow restaurant. This place was my savior when my mother didn't feed me. The bright sign loomed ahead, a beacon of comfort and a reminder of countless meals shared there. My eyes lit up.

Although I was excited to be returning home, a wave of concern washed over me. What would I tell my friends from the bus stop? They'd all moved on, their lives continuing while I had been away. The thought of explaining where I had been for the past three and a half years made my stomach twist. I felt flushed with embarrassment at the idea of sharing the details of my journey—how could I possibly convey the complexity of it all? I imagined their reactions: curiosity mixed with pity, maybe even judgment. Would they understand?

As we turned onto 90th Street and approached our house, I scanned the area, hoping not to spot anyone I might know. The familiar sights—the long row of cookie-cutter houses, the trees lining the street—felt both comforting and suffocating. As we parked, I could hear a couple of kids playing in their yards, their laughter ringing out like a reminder of what I had missed. But I turned away, the knot in my stomach tightening.

I waited on the porch for my father to open the door, feeling more like a guest than a resident.

He climbed the stairs with my suitcase in hand, and I followed, my heart pounding. As we reached the top, I spotted my grandmother; Rebecca, waiting there–tears on her cheeks. She extended her arms; and pulled me into a tight embrace. “I missed you so much,” she whispered, her voice trembling. A wave of emotion washed over me—relief, sadness, gratitude. I let myself lean into her, allowing the weight of the past few years to surface. I recalled the last time I saw her, our fingers touching through the gap in the fence before she disappeared from my life. That small gesture had felt like a lifeline, a promise that I wasn’t entirely alone.

Standing, in her embrace now, I realized how much I had longed for this connection. All those moments of separation and uncertainty melted away, if only for a heartbeat. Yet, as I pulled back to look into her eyes, I felt a mix of joy and heartache.

I turned to the living room and saw my mother sitting perfectly upright in a chair. She was dressed in her going-out attire, complete with her sleek black wig, pale white face powder, and bold red lipstick, her hands neatly folded in her lap. Her appearance was ghostly as she stared into my eyes. Tension was etched on her features, and the rigidness of her posture made it clear that she was anything but happy. I stood there, caught in the intensity of her gaze, searching for some sign of warmth or welcome. But all I saw was an unyielding expression that left me feeling exposed and vulnerable. My grandmother, sensing the tension in the air, took me by the hand and led me toward my room. As we settled onto the bed, I appreciated the warmth of her presence, a contrast to the chill in the living room.

"Are you hungry, dear?" she asked gently. I realized then that my physical appearance was probably worse than I thought. I hesitated, not wanting to burden her with the details. "Just a little," I replied. As I looked around the room, everything felt familiar—tan shag carpet, light blue walls, and my old desk containing my color pencil drawings. Memories rushed back: late nights spent drawing and dreaming. This space felt frozen in time, a reminder of who I was before everything changed.

The bed had a six-inch mattress, firm and unyielding, and no urine stains—just a crisp, clean sheet that smelled of laundry detergent.

Chapter 22

Making Change

As summer approaches and the school year winds down, the pressure to face my old bus stop friends becomes harder to ignore. Over three years had passed, and with it, a lifetime of experiences I couldn't easily explain. I still remembered the jokes, the banter, the small talk that felt so ordinary back then. Now, the idea of joining them filled me with dread. What would I say? Why had I disappeared without a word? No one ever prepared me for these kinds of moments. The words I could imagine felt either too empty or too revealing. Did I even owe them the truth?

For the first few weeks, I stayed out of sight. I'd sit behind the living room curtains, peeking through the slats, watching the neighborhood kids run around and shout to one another like nothing had changed. But everything had changed for me.

The longer I stayed hidden, the heavier the weight became. It wasn't sustainable—hiding wasn't the answer. I knew that. Eventually, the urge to stop avoiding it all overtook me. I told myself I'd make it simple. No grand story, no unnecessary details—just enough of an explanation to get by. If they asked, I'd tell them I'd been away, make it sound casual, then move on. It seemed like the safest way to protect myself from digging too deep into the truth. What happened next was up to them.

I waited until Saturday morning when everyone played in the street; this way it would be done in one shot. From my window, I watched the street come alive, filled with the shouts and laughter of kids spilling onto the pavement. Some faces were familiar, while others were new, adding to the uncertainty I felt. I descended the stairs, my palms slick with sweat.

I paused in the darkness of the foyer, my hand gripping the cold doorknob. I stood there, frozen.

Then, I stepped outside and walked down the driveway toward the street, facing them all. They were setting up for a game of stickball, choosing teams like they had done countless times before.

Suddenly, everything stopped. The game, the banter, even the sounds of the street seemed to fade as all eyes turned toward me. I could feel the weight of their attention, the curiosity and surprise hanging in the air. For a split second, I wondered if I'd made the wrong choice—if this would all end in awkward silence or worse, rejection.

But then, two of the kids broke the stillness. Smiles spread across their faces as they walked toward me, closing the distance without hesitation. Without a word, they extended their palms, waiting for me to "slap them five." It was a gesture we had done a hundred times before—but in that moment, it felt like everything.

The familiar greeting, so casual yet full of meaning, was enough to pull me back in. It wasn't about explanations or apologies. It was just about being there.

That summer in Howard Beach gave me a renewed sense of hope about the future. The weight of the past few years seemed to lighten with each day I spent with my friends. Of course, they eventually asked where I'd been. I had anticipated the question, but I wasn't eager to relive it. So, I brushed it off as best I could, keeping my answers brief.

No one pushed too hard, and soon enough, the questions faded into the background.

At home, I did my best to avoid communication with my mother. Her volatile moods made each day feel like walking on eggshells. I quickly learned how to navigate around her anger, doing whatever was necessary to stay out of her way. Most days, I spent my time locked in my room, finding peace in the quiet, or escaping outside to be with my friends. Out there, I didn't have to worry about the tension at home.

As the new school year approached in the fall of 1970, I learned that I wouldn't be attending the local public school. My parents had decided I should go to a private school instead. The news hit me like a wave of anxiety. What would it be like? Would I fit in with the other kids? The idea of navigating a new environment felt overwhelming, especially knowing I hadn't been in a classroom for years. I tried to remind myself that maybe this change could lead to new opportunities. Still, the anxiety lingered, a constant reminder of how unsteady everything felt.

Shortly after I started at the new school, I realized that the place was less about learning and more like a childcare facility. The focal point of our day wasn't in the classroom—it was on the football field. Two-hand touch football in the park was everything. Our small school had only two teachers, and it didn't really matter what subject we were supposed to be learning or whether we were under the care of Mr. Gallia or Mr. Keebler. What mattered was whose team you were on; were you a part of "Gallia's Goons," or did you line up with "Keebler's Cookies."

We were bused in, played ball, had lunch, and then returned home in the afternoon. The days blurred together in a monotonous routine, with little substance or engagement. This pattern continued through the entire school year, dragging on until the summer of 1971. I found myself yearning for something more—real challenges, meaningful connections—but each day felt like a step further away from that hope. I was left to navigate the days with a growing sense of disillusionment.

Once again, summer was upon us, and stickball ruled my days as I spent hours outdoors, eager to escape my mother's wrath.

The tension at home was something I had learned to live around, but one Saturday morning, things took a different turn. My father was home from work that day, and he asked me to join him for breakfast. We drove to a local diner and sat across from one another at a cramped table. After we placed our orders, he did something he rarely did—he made direct eye contact. "Your mother and I are getting divorced," he said, his voice calm. "We've decided that you will go with me, and your brother will stay with her." I remember feeling confused, unsure of what that meant for my life. Where would we go? What would it look like? I couldn't even begin to piece it together. Sensing my uncertainty, he added, "I'm dating a woman who lives in the Bronx. For now, we're going to live with her." I sat there, trying to absorb everything; my life, once again, was about to change.

It wasn't long before that day came. I packed my suitcase—the one that was involved in every heartbreak in my life—and left the home with my father. There were no goodbyes, no hugs or kisses, just an instruction: take your bag and go. My father and I drove with little said between us. I stole occasional glances at him, his face set in a way that told me he, too, was carrying a weight that words couldn't lift. As we approached our new home in the Bronx, a wave of unease washed over me. The buildings, with their stoops and worn facades, felt hauntingly familiar, reminiscent of Boerum Street, where I had spent over three years. We pulled up in front of a brownstone, and as we stepped out, the air was thick with the scent of street food and distant laughter.

Joan, my father's girlfriend, stood on the steps, her smile wide, almost cartoonish. Her eyes gleamed with an intensity that felt both welcoming and disquieting. As we followed her in, Joan's smile remained plastered on her face, an unyielding expression that felt both creepy and strangely familiar. I couldn't shake the unsettling feeling it stirred in me. Just as we reached the door, she turned to face us, her eyes sparkling with that same eerie enthusiasm.

In that moment, it dawned on me where I'd seen that smile before: she looked just like the Joker from the Batman series. With a splash of green hair dye, I thought she'd be a perfect match, a mix of unsettling charm and chaotic energy. I wondered if this new chapter would be more like a comic book than I'd anticipated.

Joan introduced us to her parents, who lived there as well. Her mother had warm eyes that made you feel at home. Her father was thin, his rugged, worn face telling stories of a hard life but softened by a gentle smile. I reminded myself that the crowded living arrangements were only temporary, a brief pause in the journey ahead. The atmosphere was welcoming, filled with the scent of home-cooked meals and the soft hum of conversation. For now, this would be our sanctuary.

After we settled in and received our sleeping arrangements I had a chance to think about what my role was here. I was aware that school was starting soon; but where would I go? Would I be placed in the school here? The thought sparked a surge of anxiety. At thirteen years old, I was supposed to be starting 8th grade, but the reality was that I hadn't attended school in six years. The first weekend in Joan's house, my father sat me down at the kitchen table for a talk. The table was cluttered with piles of change—quarters, dimes, nickels, pennies—mixed in with an assortment of paper money: singles, fives, tens, twenties. I looked at the spread, confused about what it all meant. My father explained that we wouldn't be living at Joan's for long, so enrolling me in the local school wasn't a great idea.

Instead, he proposed that I drive with him to work every day in Manhattan. It felt like a temporary fix, but I tried to remain open to it. His coffee shop, located on 7th Avenue and 35th Street in the Garment District, was bustling. It offered tables and stools for customers, but the real draw was the delivery service for nearby businesses. He told me I would join the delivery staff, which consisted of three Hispanic men who spoke very little English. As I listened to my father, it hit me: come fall of 1971, I would be working as a delivery boy instead of attending school. It dawned on me that I was now a thirteen year old boy with a second grade education.

My father and I spent over an hour at the kitchen table as he taught me how to make change using all the coins and bills. He drew up delivery bills with various amounts, having me calculate the change. Then he took it a step further. He presented a bill for $6.15, handed me a ten-dollar bill, and watched as I began to make the change. Just as I was about to return $4.85, he slipped me $1.15. I hesitated for a moment, then recalculated, returning a five dollar bill. It was a lesson in quick thinking and adaptability, and with each exchange, I felt more confident in my new role.

So in the fall of 1971, I became the new delivery boy at the coffee shop, earning around $20.00 a day. I quickly befriended the senior delivery guy, Victor, who was in his sixties and still ran through the streets, determined to make as many deliveries as possible. The unspoken rule was simple: whoever returned first from their delivery would snag the next order. Sometimes, we'd spot each other on the street after a drop-off and race back to the store, laughter mingling with the rush of adrenaline as we tried to outpace one another. Those moments transformed the job into a playful competition, and Victor's experience and enthusiasm made the long days feel a bit lighter.

In April of 1973, I turned fifteen years old. What had started as a temporary job delivering food had lasted a year and a half, stretching into the summer of 1973. During that time, many of my father's regular customers began to ask why I wasn't in school.

Each time, he offered the same answer: we were moving out of the area into a new home, but construction kept getting delayed. I could see the concern in their eyes, but I remained silent, resigned to my situation. As the months passed, I wondered when—or if—I would finally see the inside of a classroom and what that would mean for my future.

Every day after 2:00 PM, the restaurant would fall silent as the staff began cleaning up and preparing to close at 3:00 PM. It was during this quiet time that one of the waitresses offered me brief tutoring sessions. Sometimes we'd delve into Roman numerals, or we'd chat about history. She recognized the educational injustice I was facing and genuinely wanted to help. Those moments were a breath of fresh air amidst the routine of deliveries, igniting a spark of curiosity in me. I appreciated her kindness, knowing that she was providing me with the lessons I desperately needed, even if they were just snippets of knowledge.

During her tutoring sessions, my father would often interject, suggesting I consider joining the Army. He tried to convince me it would be a great opportunity, offering housing, food, and a solid career. At the time, I didn't fully grasp his motivations, but later I understood it as a way for him to relieve himself of any further obligations. It felt like he was looking for an easy way out. While I appreciated his concern for my future, it stung to realize he might see this as a way to distance himself from me, rather than support me in finding my own path.

Chapter 23

Here we go again!

Instead of stickball in the street, my summer now revolved around delivering food. I was making money, but I really missed the carefree days of being a kid. One morning, as I drove to work with my father, he shared some news: "Our new house is ready. We're meeting the builder this weekend." He smiled, but I just felt apprehension. It sounded exciting, but to me, it was another transition to navigate.

That Saturday, my father and I jumped into his "new" car,—a brown 1971 Buick Electra 225 to go see the new house. As we drove over the George Washington Bridge and north on the Palisades Parkway, I felt a sense of fresh adventure. This was new territory for me; replacing cramped brownstones, were wide-open spaces and green grass stretching as far as I could see.

After about thirty minutes, we exited on (8W) in Nanuet, New York and approached the new housing development. While our home was new, other parts of the community already had families living there. A community park was also being constructed, called Lake Nanuet.

My father drove slowly on the unpaved road, avoiding the protruding manhole covers. But as we approached Jockey Hollow

Drive, instead of going around the last one, he decided to straddle it. Just then the road dipped, causing the car's undercarriage to grab onto the manhole cover with a jolt. We came to a sudden stop. Exiting the car, we noticed both front fenders were dented, rendering the vehicle undrivable. With no choice, my father left the car behind and we walked to the new house to meet the builder. The house was magnificent—nicer than the one in Howard Beach. It had four bedrooms upstairs, a lovely kitchen, and a spacious yard. It seemed like my father and I had a knack for running into trouble whenever we visited new homes. First, it was the steamroller in Howard Beach that nearly killed me, and now the car was stuck on the manhole cover. I wondered what else awaited us in this new chapter.

In the next few weeks, first my father and I and then Joan moved into the new home in Nanuet. For the next couple of weeks, I continued traveling into Manhattan with my father to deliver food until he found a replacement for me. As summer wound down, I started playing basketball at a local park. Now that I lived in Rockland County, basketball became the new stickball, and I found myself enjoying it more than I expected.

Occasionally, I'd come home in the early afternoon to find Joan asleep on the couch, looking a bit disheveled. This became more common and it wasn't long before my father started discovering empty liquor bottles buried at the bottom of the trash.

Shortly thereafter, Joan moved out. My father and I were now alone in the house, which was fine with me. One evening, my father told me he had registered me at the local school. It felt like another step forward, another new beginning. I was excited to hear the news, but then reality hit. I had just turned fifteen, yet my education level was only at a third grade level. The thought of attending school with other kids my age filled me with panic and the fear of potential embarrassment. How would I fit in?

My first day at the school arrived. I was picked up by a large yellow school bus which stopped at almost every block, picking up students until it was full, before finally arriving at Nanuet Senior High School. Hundreds of kids poured out of the buses, making their way to the entrance. It felt like cattle being herded into a corral. Somehow, I ended up in the right class—which was my homeroom.

Although I was fifteen, I was labeled a high school freshman. Most freshmen were either thirteen or fourteen, navigating a new world of lockers and class schedules, while I felt like I was a step behind and yet somehow older. The difference wasn't just in age, but in the weight of the years I carried. I was more experienced in certain ways, having seen and lived through things that made the usual freshman anxieties seem small. Yet, there I was, starting over, just like them.

We were all finding our way through the maze of classrooms and cliques, and for the first time in a long while, I wasn't the only one starting over. In a strange way, this was an ideal time for me to enter. As time passed, my anxiety subsided, and the knots in my stomach began to loosen.

Academically, things were tough. I struggled with the basic learning process, my mind often drifting, trying to catch up with concepts that felt just out of reach. Each test, each homework assignment was a battle, and while others seemed to breeze through, I worked hard, often barely scraping by with a D or, on a good day, a C. It was like trying to stay afloat in a storm. But despite the difficulty, I refused to give up. What saved me from sinking completely were the after-school sports programs. I found a sense of belonging on the field. I made the football team, playing fullback and defensive tackle, roles that demanded strength and focus. Out there, it didn't matter how well I could solve for X or write an essay—what mattered was heart and effort, things I had in abundance. For the first time, I felt like I was good at something.

I made a few friends, mostly teammates but my social skills were lacking. Small talk felt awkward, as if there were a script everyone else had memorized whereas I'd never been handed a copy. Still, we shared the bond of the game, and that was enough for now. While I enjoyed playing football, the practices were grueling. The coach worked us to exhaustion—something the other kids were used to, having played for several seasons growing up. For me, it was just another steep learning curve, like everything else in this new world.

My routine settled into a steady rhythm: bus to school, football practice after class, long walk home. Most of the kids were prepared. They brought drinks, protein bars, or snacks to school, knowing they'd need energy for the day ahead. After practice all the kids would just hop into their parents car and be driven home. I didn't have that luxury. My father was generally nowhere to be found, and I learned quickly that I was on my own.

The house was empty when I woke up to get ready for school: no one to say good morning, no sound of breakfast being made, just the ticking of a clock and the rustle of my clothes as I hurried to catch the bus. Occasionally, I'd see my father's car in the driveway when I got home, but he was usually in his room with the door closed, lost in his own world.

One day, I got home early because there was no football practice. I was surprised to see my father's car parked outside so early in the day. As I stepped inside, something felt off. There was a low murmur coming from the living room. A voice—female. My heart skipped a beat. I turned the corner, and there they were, sitting on the couch, close enough that the space between them barely existed. My father, usually so reserved and distant, was smiling. A real smile, one I hadn't seen in a long time, if ever. He stood up quickly, a little awkwardly, like he hadn't expected me to walk in. "Mitchel, this is Judy," he said, gesturing to the woman.

Judy had black curly hair that framed her face, and brown eyes that flickered with something I couldn't quite place. She smiled at me, but her voice didn't carry the warmth her expression tried to project. "Hi, Mitchel," she said, her words flat, as if they were part of a script. I mumbled a hello and quickly climbed the stairs to my room. I sat on the bed, processing what I had just seen. My father, who had been a ghost in my life for so long, was suddenly animated, but it wasn't for me. It was for her.

As time passed, Judy was around more often, her laugh echoing from the living room, filling what had once been my father's silence. It wasn't long before I was introduced to her two daughters—one was thirteen, the other sixteen. Like pieces being set on a chessboard, they were being placed into my life, with no move left for me. Judy, with her bright smile and ever-present voice, was no longer just a guest. She and her daughters were scheduled to move in. Everything had shifted so quickly, as if my father's life had been playing out behind a curtain, and now it was being revealed all at once.

In some ways, Judy reminded me of Joan, playing a role with her wide smile and easy confidence. But unlike Joan, her presence felt more permanent, more inescapable. The dynamic of the house changed quickly. Judy's daughters brought new energy, new voices, and a new set of rules. I couldn't help but feel out of place, like a stranger in what had once been my refuge.

It wasn't long before my father and Judy visited town hall and made it official. Once they did, everything changed. A new sheriff was in town, and it wasn't my father. While he worked long hours, Judy took over the house, running it like her own little fiefdom. A questionable demeanor, which had been subtle at first, was now on full display.

She complained constantly. If my room wasn't up to her standards, she'd let me know with a sharp word and a withering look. If I made myself a sandwich and used what she deemed "too many" slices of cold cuts, she'd snap at me. She seemed unaware that a sixteen-year-old boy consumed more food than a thirteen-year-old girl! Every small action seemed to irritate her, and nothing I did was right in her eyes. It became clear that she wasn't interested in helping me, guiding me, or even trying to connect. I was just an obstacle—a reminder of my father's past life, perhaps, or simply a nuisance in her carefully constructed new world.

Over the next couple of years, I watched as my father fell into the same role with Judy that he had with my mother. It was a painful and frustrating déjà vu. Just as he had allowed my mother to push me out of the house to avoid her tantrums, he repeated that same lack of authority with Judy. It was as though he had surrendered again, stepping aside to keep the peace at the cost of my well-being.

Each time Judy's voice rose in complaint or frustration, I looked to him for some support or intervention, but it never came. He stayed silent, as if retreating into the same shell he had built when I was younger. When it came to conflict, my father's default was to remove himself from the equation entirely.

It became clear that I was once again on my own, left to navigate Judy's constant criticisms and control without any help from the one person I thought might stand up for me.

Chapter 24

Eating Chips in the Snow

It was the fall of 1977, and I was nineteen years old, looking forward to the future with excitement and disbelief. Graduation was right around the corner. After everything I had been through, it didn't quite feel real—I was actually going to graduate from high school.

With money from a couple of part time jobs, and what I've saved from the coffee shop, I finally had enough to buy my first car. I was now somewhat independent—no more long walks home from school, no more waiting for buses that never seemed to arrive on time. Everything was about to change for the better, I thought.

As graduation day approached, I found myself reflecting on the journey that had brought me to this moment. The senior prom was just a week away, and I was filled with excitement. It was more than just a dance; it was a celebration of our shared experiences and the culmination of years spent together. Decked out in our finest leisure suits, my friends and I couldn't help but feel a little cooler than usual. Our long hair swung in the breeze. We looked like we had just walked off the set of a 70s movie—sharp, confident, and ready for the night ahead.

The venue was transformed into a magical setting, with a dazzling disco ball spinning overhead, scattering light across the dance floor, and colorful decorations that set a vibrant mood.

Graduation day arrived, and with it the bittersweet feeling of leaving behind the familiarity of high school. Applause from friends filled the air. My name was called, I stepped forward. The moment my hand met the principal's, and I accepted my diploma, a rush of emotions flooded over me. It was a tangible symbol of my hard work and perseverance—a reminder that I had overcome challenges and reached this significant milestone. After celebrating the graduation, I returned home buzzing from the excitement of the day but also ready to let it all settle. The house was quiet. My father hadn't returned from work yet, and Judy was out, leaving behind a stillness that, for once, felt welcoming.

I went to bed early, the memories of my graduation replaying in my mind like a highlight reel.

The next morning, I woke to the familiar sounds of disagreements between my father and Judy. It was Saturday, and that meant my father was home. His voice mingled with Judy's, the tone unmistakably tense.

Their conversations often started quietly enough, but they rarely stayed that way for long. I had grown used to the rhythm of it—the way the tension would build and the volume would rise until it became background noise I tried to ignore. But this morning, it felt sharper, more immediate, as if it were cutting through the walls.

After showering and getting dressed, I realized the banter had stopped. The house was suddenly quiet, which was almost as unsettling as the noise. I made my way down the stairs, and I slipped out the side door to my car, eager to escape the tension inside. Just as I reached for the car door, the garage door opened and my father stepped out. His head was low, his posture slumped, as if he carried the weight of something heavy. I paused, expecting a routine exchange, but when he looked up at me, his eyes seemed different.

"I heard you graduated yesterday," he said, his voice quiet but pointed. "Congratulations." There was a pause, a moment where I felt the slightest flicker of pride, but before I could respond, he continued. "With this comes responsibility." I stood there, not quite sure where he was headed, but sensed something was off. As he spoke, I noticed movement behind the side door—the curtain shifted, and there was Judy, watching us through the window, her eyes fixed on the unfolding scene.

"You're now a man," my father stated, his voice firmer this time, with a strange finality to it. "It's time for you to move." The words hit me like a punch to the gut. I couldn't believe what was happening. After everything, after surviving all the chaos and finally reaching graduation, he was getting rid of me again. There was no conversation, no plan, just a cold, matter-of-fact statement. It was up to me now—to figure it out, to survive on my own. I stared at him, searching for something in his face—a hint of remorse, or at least some recognition of the gravity of what he was saying—but all I saw was the same resigned expression he had worn through most of my life. I was on my own. Again.

What started out as a laid-back Saturday, a day I had planned to bask in the quiet satisfaction of my personal victory—finally graduating from high school—was now unraveling into yet another battle for survival. I sat in my car, gripping the steering wheel, my mind racing as I tried to piece together a solution to this new and unexpected hurdle. The shock of my father's words still lingered, and now I had to face the reality that my home was no longer mine. Where would I go? What would I do next? First, my thoughts drifted to my mother, who lived in a cramped apartment in Queens with my brother. The idea of calling her flashed in my mind as a potential option, but it immediately felt like a last resort—a desperate move I didn't want to make unless I had no other choice.

I slammed the car into gear and pulled out of the driveway, not caring where I ended up. Before I knew it, I found myself in Spring Valley, a rundown area I was familiar with only by reputation.

It was a place known for its poverty, a town where people struggled to make ends meet. The buildings were old, worn down by years of neglect, and the streets were filled with individuals who, like me, were just trying to survive.

As I continued driving down one of the side streets, something caught my eye—a large, weathered two-story home with a sign in the yard that read, "Rentals Available." The house stood out, not just because of the sign, but also because there was a police car parked out front. A uniformed officer was talking with a middle-aged white man who stood on the front entrance porch, his arms crossed and his face set in a grim expression.

I parked the car, took a deep breath, and I walked up the cracked, uneven pathway toward the front porch. The officer had just turned to leave, and the man on the porch locked eyes with me as I approached. "Can I help you?" he asked sharply, as though my presence was just another inconvenience in his day. His gaze was hard, sizing me up. "I'm looking to rent an apartment," I said, trying to keep my voice steady. I wasn't sure what kind of impression I was making as this whole situation was foreign to me. I had no idea what it cost to rent an apartment, and my savings.

His expression softened, slightly. "Sure," he replied, "Let me show you what I've got." He waved for me to follow him inside. Stepping across the threshold, I was immediately hit by a musty, stale odor. The interior was dimly lit, and the air felt thick, as if the place hadn't been aired out in ages. The wallpaper was peeling and the carpet underfoot was threadbare, with stains that looked like they'd been there longer than I'd been alive.

"This here's a shared house," the man said as we walked down a hallway, passing several closed doors. "Got a couple of rooms open on the second floor. Bathrooms are shared, and no cooking in the rooms. You work? You'll need the first and last month's rent upfront." I nodded, trying to keep up with the rapid-fire information. I wondered if I could even afford it. He glanced back at me, his eyes narrowing, as if trying to gauge if I was serious. The stairs creaked loudly as we ascended, and I wondered what kind of people lived here. The house felt like it had stories to tell, none of them particularly good. When we reached the second floor, he pushed open a door to one of the rooms; the small space had a bed that sagged in the middle, and a dresser that looked like it might fall apart if I touched it.

"This one's available," he said. "It's thirty-five dollars a month." I swallowed hard. "It's… uh, it's not bad," I stammered. "I'll take it." I returned home, my mind still reeling from the whirlwind of the day. I went straight to the garage and found an old, cardboard box; hauled it to my room and began piling in my clothes—shirts, jeans, socks. As I packed, I looked around the room, memories flooding back. This had been my space, my small corner of the world. But now, I was leaving, and part of me felt relieved. I could finally escape the weight that had been building since Judy entered the picture.

Stuffing the last of my clothes into the box, I turned to my black-and-white television, the one thing I owned that felt like a real connection to some semblance of comfort. Without hesitation, I unplugged it from the wall, gently removing the rabbit ears, and carried it downstairs.

I made my way to the car, balancing the box and TV. I glanced back at the house one last time. The sense of finality hit me–this chapter was closing, and I wasn't sure what lay ahead. I made my way back to Spring Valley. The large, slightly rundown building looked even more daunting now that it would be my home. I parked in the same spot and found the man I had spoken to earlier, standing near his small office by the front door. I pulled out the check I had written for seventy dollars—first and last month's rent—and handed it to him, my hand steady but my mind swirling. He fished the apartment key from his pocket and handed it to me. "Welcome," he muttered, already turning back toward his office. I stood there for a moment, gripping the cold metal key, feeling the weight of it in my hand. This was it. My new life, however uncertain, was beginning right here.

Within an hour my clothes were folded and placed in the musty wooden dresser that I had repurposed as a TV stand. It wobbled slightly but it held. I had taken a few essentials from my home in Nanuet—an old sheet and a couple of towels. I spread the sheet across the worn mattress that had been left behind, not bothering to make it neat. It was enough for now.

The place smelled of dust and mildew, the kind of odor that clings to old, forgotten buildings. But it didn't matter. I was free, or at least as free as I had ever been. There was a strange comfort in the simplicity of it all. No loud arguments, no Judy hovering over me with her constant criticisms—just silence. For the first time in a long while, I sat down on the edge of the bed, looking around the room. It wasn't much, but it was mine, and for that, I was grateful. Before the sun dipped below the horizon, I decided to step outside and get a feel for the neighborhood.

As I walked, the reality of where I was living began to settle in. The area was a mix of broken-down single-family homes—some with boarded-up windows—and relatively new brownstone apartment complexes, which stood out against the decay around them. The streets were quiet, eerily so, with no kids playing outside, no people walking their dogs, no sign of any community life. Just a few scattered figures who moved quickly and silently, as if they had somewhere more important to be.

I kept walking, hoping to find something, anything, that resembled a grocery store or a diner, but it soon became clear there were none within walking distance. A car was a necessity here, and I was thankful I had mine. Still, there was a feeling of isolation in the air—a sense that this part of Spring Valley was where people came when they had nowhere else to go.

To make ends meet, I juggled two jobs—one at Ander's Men's Wear on Route 59 in Nanuet, a men's clothing store, and the other at "Penny-Back Jeans" in the Nanuet Mall. While I was grateful for the employment, my salary was barely enough to cover my expenses. As I made my way back to my building, I glanced up at the dimming sky, the street lights flickering on, casting long shadows across the cracked sidewalks. This was my world now, and as foreign and rough as it seemed, it was the next step in my journey. In bed, I turned on the TV, grateful that I could get a decent signal after some fiddling with the rabbit ears. But the tranquility was shattered by the sounds of chaos outside my door. Suddenly, the building came alive with the sounds of people arriving—doors slamming, voices raised in argument, and others shouting in animated discussions, many of them in Spanish. I couldn't decipher what they were saying. As night fell, the atmosphere darkened.

I heard the sharp crack of glass shattering followed by slurred speech echoing in the hallway. Panic settled in my stomach like a stone. I turned off the TV, the comforting noise replaced by the unnerving reality just outside my door. I edged my way to the floor, my back against the solid surface of the door, feeling every beat of my heart pounding in my ears. I tensed, praying that whatever was happening would stay outside. I could hear shouting, the clamor of voices rising and falling, I felt utterly isolated. My new apartment, which had promised a sense of independence, now felt like a cage. I wrapped my arms around my knees, listening intently, hoping that the chaos would die down soon. The night felt endless, and as I sat in that quiet darkness, I felt that I was now a part of something much bigger and more dangerous than I had anticipated.

After an hour I tried to close my eyes and fall asleep only to be jarred awake by the sounds of breaking glass. I needed to urinate but was too afraid to open my door. I urinated in a paper cup and left it in the corner of my room.

The scene that greeted me in the morning was a chilling reflection of the chaos from the night before. The hallway was littered with shards of broken glass, and my eyes widened as I noticed bloody footprints on the floor. Bloody handprints trailed down the hall, a macabre path that sent shivers down my spine. Navigating around the debris, I headed to the bathroom. It was as grimy as I had feared. It housed only a toilet, a sink, and a single shower stall, whose plastic curtain was thick with mildew. The floor was a mosaic of cracked black and white tiles, marred further by the remnants of vomit from the previous night's festivities.

As the days turned into weeks, I started to piece together the rhythm of life in the building. During the week, the tenants hustled tirelessly, putting in long hours at low-paying jobs, all in the desperate bid to make ends meet. The streets were filled with people rushing to and from work, faces drawn with fatigue yet determined to provide for their families. But come the weekend, the atmosphere shifted dramatically.

The same individuals who had toiled hard all week transformed, shedding their burdens for a time. They would gather in the hallways, laughter mingling with shouts, music blaring from open windows. It was as if the weight of their daily struggles exploded in a riotous release. I learned quickly that the weekends were a dangerous time—where laughter could turn into aggression in an instant, and where I had to remain vigilant just to survive.

After paying rent, gas, and auto insurance, along with basic necessities like food, it became increasingly clear that survival was going to be a constant struggle. Each week was a balancing act; if I spent even a couple of dollars more than usual, I risked falling short on my rent. The anxiety of financial instability loomed over me. I tried every possible way to save—eating less, cutting down on gas by coasting in neutral—but it always felt like I was on the verge of slipping through thc cracks. Despite the challenges, I held onto a flicker of hope. I was determined to carve out a life for myself, one that would eventually lead to something better.

As the cool days of fall gave way to the biting cold of winter, I quickly realized that my apartment was no refuge from the harsh weather. It felt no warmer inside than on the frozen streets outside. The building had little insulation, and heat was either nonexistent or barely noticeable. I found myself bundling up in the same clothes I wore outside, keeping on my coat and sometimes even gloves while sitting in my room. The cold crept in from every corner—through the cracks in the windows, under the door, and from the thin walls that did little to block out the freezing air. Each night was a battle to stay warm.

The day before my rent was due, the county was hit with a massive snow storm, leaving cars buried in snow. As I watched the snow pile up, hunger gnawed at me. My stomach twisted painfully, and the dizziness from not eating clouded my thoughts. It was as though the storm had trapped me in more than just snow—it had imprisoned me in my own desperation. I had just three dollars in my pocket, and with rent looming, it felt like I was already losing. I knew I had to get to a store, despite the blizzard. It was only a five-minute drive away, but with my car buried under snow and no gas to spare, walking was my only option. I bundled up as best as I could. The snow was relentless, pushing against me with every stride, and the cold bit through my clothes. The world seemed so much bigger and more desolate under the weight of the storm.

What would have taken a few minutes in a car stretched into an exhausting, forty-minute trek. Each step was a struggle against the wind and the mounds of snow, and as I pushed forward, I could feel the strength draining from my body. The dizziness from hunger mixed with the cold, making the journey feel endless. I kept moving, hoping that I could make it to the store before I collapsed. As I entered the store, the warm air hit my face, momentarily easing the sting of the biting cold. My breathing steadied, and I counted the three crumpled dollars in my pocket. My plan was to buy enough food to last through the day, but with only three dollars in my pocket, that was a stretch.

I ended up purchasing a large bag of chips, a drink, and a pack of Yankee Doodles. Although the Yankee Doodles were symbolic, reminding me of my father's visits to Childville, I still savored them. Before I even reached the halfway point on my walk home, I had already finished them along with the drink.

My stomach felt a bit more settled, and as I trudged through the snow, I opened the bag of chips, hoping they'd hold me over for the rest of the day. By the time I reached the front porch, the bag was empty, and I tilted it up, shaking the last bits of chip dust into my mouth, desperate to make the most of what little I had.

The struggle I faced during that brutal winter was the turning point. It became clear that if I was ever going to achieve any sort of financial comfort, I needed to make some serious changes. Surviving on the bare minimum, constantly on the verge of falling behind, wasn't sustainable. The cold, hunger, and the weight of barely making it had pushed me to my limit. I realized I couldn't continue living like this—I had to find a new path, one that would offer more stability and security.

Chapter 25

The Final Chapter

While in high school, I briefly entertained the idea of becoming a police officer. I had always disliked bullies and couldn't stand to see people being taken advantage of; I'm sure this was due to my experiences at Childville.

In my mind, police officers were the ones who helped level the playing field, protecting the vulnerable and standing up for what was right. The thought of making a difference, stepping in when others couldn't, resonated with me. It seemed like a way to channel my desire for fairness and justice into something meaningful. I thought my chances of getting hired by the police department would be better in New York City, given the higher demand for officers. To improve my chances, I decided to enroll in John Jay College of Criminal Justice.

It felt like the logical step toward making my goal a reality. However, I was apprehensive. The idea of competing at a college level made me doubt myself, as I wasn't sure if I had what it took to succeed academically. The thought of stepping into a new environment filled with ambitious students was intimidating, but I knew I had to give it a try if I wanted to pursue this path. The only way the plan could work was if I lived closer to New York City. The thought of calling my mother, let alone asking to move into her small apartment in Queens, filled me with anxiety. Every conversation with her seemed to bring stress, and the idea of being back in that environment was almost unbearable. But I knew I had few options, and moving closer to the city was essential if I wanted to make college and the police force a reality. It felt like I was trading one challenge for another, but I was willing to take that risk for a shot at a better future.

The next day, I made the call to my mother, trying to explain why this move was so important to me. My stomach was in knots, anticipating her reaction. Surprisingly, after a brief pause, she responded with a simple "yes."

No questions, no arguments—just her agreement. It wasn't the warmest response, but it was an answer, and it meant I could move forward. I hung up, feeling a strange mix of relief and uncertainty, knowing that this next chapter would come with its own set of challenges. In January of 1978, I packed up my clothes and the black-and-white TV, leaving the apartment in Spring Valley behind as I headed for my mother's place in Queens.

Shortly after my 20th birthday, I registered at John Jay College in the spring of 1978 and began taking classes. It was a new world for me, filled with both challenges and opportunities.

I quickly learned that in addition to taking classes I could sign up for internship programs that offered three college credits. I signed up for an internship with the Taxi and Limousine Commission at

Kennedy Airport. On the first day, I realized that commuting to Kennedy from college was not going to be straightforward.

Once there the students gathered for a briefing at the Port Authority Police Department on their responsibilities in maintaining safety at the airport. It was eye-opening to learn about the critical functions they perform behind the scenes. In closing, the captain announced that for anyone interested in becoming a Port Authority Police Officer, today was the final day to pick up an application at the World Trade Center.

While it was all quite fascinating, I realized I had never even heard of the Port Authority Police until today. As I rode back to the college, the train conductor announced, “Next stop: World Trade Center.” I was already set to take the New York City Police test that month and felt exhausted, but when the train pulled into the station and the doors opened, something compelled me to step off. I walked toward One World Trade Center and took the elevator up to the Port Authority Human Resources department to grab the application.

Before taking the New York City police test, I submitted my application for employment with both the Port Authority and the New York State Troopers. The morning of the police test, I felt a wave of nerves, worried that I wouldn’t perform well enough to secure the job.

A few weeks later the results arrived. The thrill of seeing that I scored a 90 on the test quickly dissolved into disbelief, as I was told that I had failed. It felt like a cruel twist of fate. In 1979, there was a push for diversity in the workforce, especially in a city as dynamic as New York. I understood the importance of affirmative action—how it aimed to correct historical injustices and create opportunities for those who had been marginalized, and that I belonged to a category that was not favored in the push for diversity. Yet, in that moment, I felt invisible, as if all my hard work and dedication were overshadowed by the category I belonged to. I wondered how many others like me were caught in this tug-of-war between merit and representation. It was a bitter pill to swallow, and I was left grappling with feelings of frustration and confusion.

In the spring of 1980 I decided to remain at John Jay College, letting nature take its course. A couple of months later, I received a letter in the mail from the Port Authority. "Congratulations, you have been accepted into the next police academy class." I could hardly believe it—after all the waiting and setbacks, I was finally being offered a chance to pursue my dreams. The words "congratulations" echoed in my mind, and I held the letter tightly. This was more than just an acceptance; it was an opportunity to transform my life. Two days later I received a letter from the New York State Police. "Congratulations, you have been accepted into the next police academy class." Standing there with both letters felt amazing.

Each opportunity was a significant milestone, and I knew that choosing between the two would shape my future in profound ways. My twenty-one-year old brain made the decision and chose the Port Authority. This turned out to be the best decision of my life.

Graduating from the Port Authority Police Academy in the spring of 1980 marked a turning point in my life. I served for 26 years before retiring in 2006. This career saved me from the constant financial hardships and uncertainty of my earlier years. Shortly after retiring, I transitioned into a new career with AIG, conducting federal background investigations for individuals seeking top-secret clearance jobs. It was a different kind of work; that allowed me to use my investigative skills. I shifted to a private security company and then another firm. Each step stabilized my post-retirement life.

Working with colored pencils, initially a therapeutic outlet for me, became a way to relax and unwind. I continued using this artistic expression, carefully crafting each piece and quietly hanging them on the walls of my home. For a long time; I kept my artwork private, content with the quiet satisfaction it brought me. The process itself was enough, providing a sense of calm in a world that often felt chaotic.

In 2015, I was encouraged to enter an art exhibition where the gallery leaders would vote on which artists would be accepted to display their work. I submitted two of my pieces, "Waiting" and "New Year's Day," and to my surprise, they won. That marked the beginning of my journey with the gallery, where I remained for over seven years, showcasing my artwork and continuing to grow as an artist. It opened new doors and gave me confidence in my creative expression.

"Waiting"

"New Year's Day"

Working for the Port Authority Police led me to become a first responder on 9/11. I spent several weeks at Ground Zero, aiding in recovery efforts. During this time, I carried a small pocket camera, capturing images of the devastation I witnessed. One particular photo stayed with me, and 17 years later, in 2018, I decided it was time to create a piece based on that photo. The result was *"The Search for Heroes,"* which was accepted into the World Trade Center Memorial Museum, becoming a part of their permanent collection. This work is a deeply personal reflection of my experience during that tragic time.

"The Search for Heroes"

After joining the Port Authority Police Department in 1980, I've been blessed with many positive experiences that have shaped my life. The most significant blessing, by far, has been my marriage to Iris. Over the years, she has played an integral role in helping me grow and mature into the man I am today. Her love and support have been constant, and together we've built a strong partnership and family. We've now been married for thirty-one years, and I couldn't imagine my life without her.

Just before my marriage to Iris, my mother, Helen, came up to visit me in Orange County, New York. It was the summer of 1992, and everything seemed to be falling into place for the future.

One afternoon, we found ourselves sitting on a park bench in Monroe, the quiet hum of summer all around us—birds chirping, the breeze moving gently through the trees, kids laughing in the distance. It felt peaceful, like any ordinary moment between mother and son, but what came next shattered that calm.

Out of nowhere, my mother turned to me, her expression softer than usual. Her eyes, which so often held something back, seemed open in a way I wasn't used to. "I'm sorry," she said. I looked at her, confused, unsure of what she was referring to. "Sorry?" I asked. She sighed deeply, and for a moment, it seemed like she was searching for the right words. "About everything I've done," she finally replied, her voice heavy with regret.

I sat there, stunned, the weight of her words settling in. I had never expected to hear those words from her. All the years of tension, the unspoken pain, the things that had gone unsaid between us—they seemed to hang in the air. I didn't know how to respond, or if I even should. It felt like we were both standing on the edge of something big, but neither of us knew how to cross over it. The breeze kept blowing, the park still buzzing with life, but in that moment, it felt like the world had stopped just for us.

CHILDVILLE

130 Boerum Street, Williamsburg, Brooklyn NY.

Mitch Rosen's Color Pencil Art

MitchRosenArt.com

Made in the USA
Columbia, SC
13 May 2025

57856195R10096